Jobs, Gender and Small Enterprise in Africa

Tanzanian Women Entrepreneurs: Going for Growth

April, 2003

**ILO Office, Dar es Salaam and
Ministry of Industry & Trade — SME Section
in association with**
InFocus Programme on Boosting Employment
through Small Enterprise Development
International Labour Office · Geneva

ILO
Tanzanian Women Entrepreneurs: Going for Growth
Geneva, International Labour Office, 2003

ISBN 92-2-113731-7

Printed in Switzerland

Foreword

Within the Department of Job Creation and Enterprise Development (EMP/ENT), the InFocus Programme on Boosting Employment through Small Enterprise Development (IFP/SEED) is the ILO's major programme to promote employment creation for women and men through small enterprise development. IFP/SEED gives priority to a number of cross-cutting aspects, including "enhancing employment opportunities for women". IFP/SEED has a team engaged on Women's Entrepreneurship Development and Gender Equality (known as WEDGE), which has been conducting research on the theme of Jobs, Gender and Small Enterprises in Africa – specifically in Ethiopia, Tanzania and Zambia.

Throughout 2002 a comprehensive review was undertaken to examine the factors affecting women entrepreneurs in each of the three countries. The first stage involved recruiting teams of national consultants, commissioning research and conducting literature reviews to capture the known facts regarding women entrepreneurs. This resulted in the publication of a set of three Preliminary Reports (ILO, October 2002) which summarized key findings from the secondary research and highlighted critical areas for further research. In Tanzania the research was conducted by University of Dar es Salaam Entrepreneurship Centre (UDEC). The next stage involved a field survey of 128 women entrepreneurs from Dar es Salaam, Arusha and Zanzibar to dig deeper and probe these critical issues, particularly as they affect women entrepreneurs' motivations, economic opportunities, and passages to growth and formalization. The transitional process of informal sector operators formalizing and becoming registered business entities is of interest and concern to the ILO.

Once the field research was completed, a national conference was organized at which the significant survey findings were presented and possible interventions proposed. Resulting from the highly participatory consultative process at the national conference held in Dar es Salaam in November 2002, a set of issues and recommendations for follow-up actions emerged. This ILO report is the culmination of the research and consultations that took place throughout 2002, and it summarizes the key issues from the secondary research, describes and analyses the survey findings, and presents recommendations from the national consultative process.

In the Tanzanian survey, the 128 women entrepreneurs have created 983 jobs, of which 752 are full-time paid jobs (an average of 5.9 per enterprise), thus demonstrating that women entrepreneurs can be a significant force in employment creation, both for family members and others. Most of the women entrepreneurs (67 per cent) used their personal savings at the start-up stage and, significantly, 79 per cent use their savings to finance the growth of their enterprises. This highlights the "missing middle" in sources of finance, as women are able to access small amounts of micro-finance, and larger enterprises are able to obtain loans from the commercial banks. Yet those women micro-entrepreneurs who want to expand their businesses from micro and small or large enterprises have difficulty obtaining appropriate amounts of funding to finance their growth plans. Only one-quarter of the women entrepreneurs are members of women's business associations, and a further 7 per cent are members of chambers and other organizations. They cite "lack of awareness" as the main reason for not joining associations. These and other significant findings from the report currently inform the ILO's programme of work in support of women entrepreneurs in Tanzania.

The entire research process conducted by the IFP/SEED's WEDGE team, and the final set of recommendations for practical actions, make a significant contribution towards the ILO's Jobs in Africa (JIA) programme and its Global Employment Agenda, particularly in relation to promoting gender equality and women's entrepreneurship as a positive "force of change". The evolving partnership with the Ministry of Industry and Trade and its SME Section, will ensure that the ILO's support to women's entrepreneurship in Tanzania makes a positive contribution to the implementation of the new SME Policy (as adopted on 11 February 2003), as well as to the implementation of the PRSP process. The enhanced knowledge base on women entrepreneurs and the practical follow-up actions also contribute significantly to women's empowerment, as indicated in the Millennium Development Goals (Goal 3, Target 4, Indicator 11).

In Tanzania this secondary and primary research was conducted by University of Dar es Salaam Entrepreneurship Centre (UDEC) under the leadership of Dr. Marcellina Chijoriga. The national research team was greatly assisted by the ILO's team of international consultants from Westfield Consultancy (Newcastle, UK), Ms. Rhona Howarth and Dr. Pat Richardson. Within the ILO, the research project was initiated, designed and supervised by Mr. Gerry Finnegan, Senior Specialist in Women's Entrepreneurship Development, with assistance from Ms. Grania Mackie (IFP/SEED). The ILO Office in Dar es Salaam has supported this process throughout 2002, and particular mention is made of the assistance provided by Mr. Morten Lehmann, Programme Officer. The ILO is also grateful to the Ministry of Industry and Trade, SME Section, for its eagerness to support and partner ILO's activities in Tanzania.

The ILO would like to acknowledge the financial support provided from the Irish Government under the ILO-Ireland Aid Partnership Programme, as well as the encouragement received from the Embassy of Ireland in Dar es Salaam, and from the Charge d'Affaires, Mr Ronan Corvin.

Ali Ibrahim
Director
ILO Office
Dar es Salaam, Tanzania

Michael Henriques
Director
Job Creation and Enterprise Development
Department (EMP/ENT)
ILO, Geneva

Table of Contents

Tables:

Acronyms and Abbreviations

BDS	Business Development Services
EOTF	Equal Opportunities for all Trust Fund
FAWETA	Federation of Women Entrepreneurs in Tanzania
FCM	Faculty of Commerce and Management
HIV/AIDS	Human Immuno-Defficiency Virus/Acquired Immune Deficiency Syndrome
IFP	InFocus Programme
ILO	International Labour Organization
MFI(s)	Micro-Finance Institution(s)
MSE(s)	Micro and Small Enterprise(s)
NBS	National Bureau of Statistics
NGO(s)	Non-Governmental Organization(s)
SEED	Boosting Employment through Small EnterprisE Development
SIDO	Small Industries Development Organization
SUWATA	Shirika la Uchumi la Wanawake Tanzania
TAFOPA	Tanzania Food Processing Association
TCCIA	Tanzania Chamber of Commerce, Industry and Agriculture
TBS	Tanzania Bureau of Standards
TGT	Tanzania Gatsby Trust
UDEC	University of Dar es Salaam Entrepreneurship Centre
UDSM	University of Dar es Salaam
UNIDO	United Nations Industrial Development Organization
VETA	Vocational Education and Training Authority
VIBINDO	Viwanda na Biashara Ndogondogo
WEDGE	Women's Entrepreneurship Development and Gender Equality

Abstract

This report on "Tanzanian Women Entrepreneurs: Going for Growth" presents the conclusions and final set of recommendations based on outcomes from field research and a national conference organized by the ILO. The field research covered 128 women entrepreneurs from Arusha, Dar es Salaam and Zanzibar, as well as further in-depth interviews with 15 women entrepreneurs. The recommendations are the result of a consultative process undertaken at the ILO's National Symposium on Women Entrepreneurs in Tanzania, held in November 2002.

The 128 women entrepreneurs in the survey have made a significant contribution to employment. They created 983 jobs for themselves and others, of which 752 are full-time, paid jobs (average of 5.9 per enterprise). The women have difficulties in accessing appropriate amounts of finance to enable them to establish and expand their enterprises, as 67 per cent depend on personal savings at start-up, and 79 per cent at the growth stage. They also see "financial ability" as an important and helpful contribution to the growth of their enterprises. Many women expand and grow by developing multiple enterprises: 30 per cent of the sample operate two enterprises, and 16 per cent have more than 2 enterprises. Out of the sample, 73 per cent had been in employment or in self-employment prior to starting their business, demonstrating that for many of the women enterprise development is a preferred career option, rather than a survival mechanism. Many women cite lack of awareness about associations as their reason for not being members, and only 25 per cent are in associations that mainly target women, while a further 7 per cent are in other business associations. The women entrepreneurs seem to be aware of the importance of job quality in managing and maintaining their workforce. There have incremental improvements in some job quality issues between the time of start-up and the present day. Furthermore, many more women entrepreneurs indicated their willingness to make additional improvements in job quality aspects.

The ILO and Ministry of Industry and Trade SME Section are collaborating to implement many of the recommendations arising from the overall research and consultation process carried out during 2002. In this way, the ILO-driven research process throughout 2002 will contribute to the implementation of the new SME Policy, as adopted by Parliament on 11 February 2003.

Executive Summary

I. Introduction

(i) Background, Objectives and Methodology of the Study

In January 2002 the International Labour Organization's InFocus Programme on Boosting Employment through Small Enterprise Development (IFP/SEED) commissioned a study on the factors affecting women entrepreneurs in creating meaningful and sustainable jobs in Tanzania, Zambia and Ethiopia. The University of Dar es Salaam Entrepreneurship Centre (UDEC) was commissioned to carry out the study in Tanzania. The study was in two phases: a secondary research stage, followed by a primary research phase.

The first stage of the research in Tanzania (April–June 2002) involved a thorough review of the secondary sources of information. Particular emphasis was placed on identifying existing documentation in the areas of micro and small enterprise development, women and gender issues, and women's entrepreneurship development. Based on this literature review, a "Preliminary report" was prepared for each country, in which key areas for further investigation were highlighted (UDEC, 2002).

The desk-based secondary research in Tanzania identified a number of obstacles to the performance of women entrepreneurs. These included limited human capacity in terms of skills and knowledge; limited access to support services, including finance, technical and management training; limited advocacy capacity; and a cultural environment which makes it more difficult for women to start and run enterprises. Despite these problems, some women manage to develop from informal economic activities at the micro level to formal small and medium enterprises, and in the process demonstrate "upward mobility". However, there is no information on how these women manage to do so given the constraints that they face.

The objective of the primary research phase of the study was to understand the processes and critical factors for women in developing small enterprises, including formalising them. The study examined the incidence of upward mobility, and strategies adopted by women who experienced upward mobility, as well as the role of the external environment in this process. The primary research comprised a sample survey of 128 women in Arusha, Dar es Salaam and Zanzibar, followed by a further in-depth study of 15 women entrepreneurs, in three sectors dominated by women: food processing, textile and leather, and beauty care,. The in-depth study examined in detail the experiences of women entrepreneurs who had achieved various levels of success.

Once the fieldwork was completed, the team of national consultants prepared a draft report based on the findings of the primary research, and presented their conclusions and a set of their draft proposed interventions. The early findings from the fieldwork and the accompanying proposals from the team of national consultants were then brought forward to a national conference that took place on 22 November 2002. At the national conference, participants were asked to take account of the results of the primary research and to consider the consultants' set of recommendations (as presented in the "proposed interventions" in Chapter 6 at the end of this report). Following the participatory consultations at the national conference, a list of key issues, priorities and recommendations was compiled.

This conference and consultative process comprised the third stage of the research process. The production of the final report, including the findings from the primary research, the consultants' set of proposed interventions, and the outcomes from the national conference, make up the final stage of the ILO's research process on women entrepreneurs in Tanzania. The outcomes from the Dar es Salaam conference are given in Chapter 7 of this report. These recommendations serve to inform the ongoing work of the ILO's IFP/SEED programme and its team engaged on Women's Entrepreneurship Development and Gender Equality (WEDGE) in Tanzania. They also form the basis of the Action Programme for 2003-2004 prepared between the ILO and the Ministry of Industry and Trade SME Section.

II. Key Findings from the Tanzanian Research

(i) Motivation and process of starting business

Most of the women entrepreneurs are engaged in business as a way of creating employment for themselves. Other motives include supplementing income, security, enjoyment of the work they are doing, use of existing competencies, and doing business as a hobby. Most start informal activities at home either as hobbies or means of meeting household needs, and later develop these into serious business activities. Early socialization and role models play a big part in motivating women to start business. Factors helpful in starting and developing businesses include skills and competencies acquired prior to starting the business, non-financial and non-financial support from family and friends, and availability of capital, equipment and working tools.

(ii) Incidence of Upward Mobility

Women entrepreneurs in the three sectors have experienced significant upward mobility in terms of formalization, employment growth, type of premises and equipment used, and size of businesses established, etc. The 128 women have created 983 jobs. Some operate more than one business in order to diversify risks, ensure a constant flow of income, or as a way of growing. Others decide to concentrate on one activity in order to effectively manage it, along with family responsibilities. Most of the women intend to make new investments, recruit more workers, and expand the range of products in the near future. Factors that have facilitated growth include access to finance; advice given by friends and relatives; moral support and encouragement from spouses, friends and family members; competencies acquired prior to starting the business, and various strategies adopted by the women entrepreneurs themselves.

(iii)   Access to and Impact of Business Support Services

(a)   Training and technical services. A number of the women involved in food processing have received technical and business management training. However, access to business skills training is often limited by lack of awareness of existing training opportunities as well as limited time available for the women to attend the training. There are not many local institutions offering training on beauty care and fashion design, and hence women in these sectors are sometimes forced to go to other countries to acquire the skills or recruit skilled employees.

(b)   Marketing, information and advisory services. Some women entrepreneurs lack the skills and information required for them to take full advantage of market opportunities. The few who have participated in trade fairs have seen significant positive impacts on their businesses as a result. Very few of the 128 women have made use of commercial advertising services.

(c)   Business associations: Awareness and membership to business associations is low. Several of the women involved in food processing are members of TAFOPA which facilitates access to packaging materials, training and trade fairs. Without this support, most of the food processing businesses in this study would not have started or survived. However, very few of the women in tailoring and beauty care have joined associations. Some have negative attitudes towards associations, while others are unaware of the existence or importance of the associations.

(iv)   Constraints to Upward Mobility

Constraints to upward mobility of the women-owned MSEs include limited access to finance, bureaucracy, competition, harassment and corruption by licensing and tax officials, perceived unfair tax levels and tax enforcement procedures, and time taken in fulfilling social/cultural responsibilities such as funerals by both the owners and employees. For growing MSEs the main problem is being able to access loans appropriate to the size of their enterprises. This is because the relatively large loans they need are not available from MFIs and most of the women lack the collateral demanded by banks.

Most of those in food processing are unable to formalize their businesses because of stringent health and hygiene requirements in terms of premises. Those in tailoring and beauty care face stiff competition in recruiting the few skilled tailors and beauticians in Tanzania and as a result of the bureaucratic procedures encountered when trying to recruit foreign workers.

Gender-related problems cited include women entrepreneurs being subjected to pressure to offer sexual favours to corrupt government officials; lack of property rights over assets which could be pledged as collateral (even being disallowed to use own properties as collateral!); lack of confidence in women by bank officers; discouragement from men when starting or formalising businesses, and inadequate management cover during maternity leave. Sometimes clients and suppliers require that the women entrepreneurs' spouses make decisions. Finally, cultural values restrict women from socialising in the business context with men, and hence from broadening their networks that could be useful in business.

(v)   Women's Strategies for Success

To overcome the various challenges that they face, women entrepreneurs who have become upwardly mobile have adopted a number of effective strategies. These include:

(a)   Financing: To address the problem of collateral, some women have been using friend's properties to pledge as collateral while others have been strategically building up assets (e.g., fixed deposit, equipment) gradually and then using them as collateral. To deal with the problems of costly procedures and small loans from MFIs, some started borrowing small sums and repaying the capital and interest quickly in order to graduate to bigger loan sizes, which is what they need to develop their businesses. Others have used their trusted assistants to attend the frequent borrowers' meetings. They have also tried to minimize the need for external financing through very careful management of cash.

(b)   Marketing: Many of the upwardly mobile women have been developing a knowledge of needs and tastes of their customers; maintaining quality; advertising their services in mass media; attending trade fairs; recruiting and retaining highly qualified staff (sometimes from outside the country), and motivating their employees to deliver the best service possible. To circumvent the high cost of advertising in mass media, some have used greeting cards as a means of advertising.

(c)   Dealing with unfriendly laws, regulations and bureaucracy: Some of the successful women have demonstrated firmness when confronted with officials who harass them. They have kept good records of financial performance and used these to convince tax officials of their appropriate tax liabilities. In some cases, they have had to engage in bribing the officials. Some have been operating informally until they were able to meet licensing requirements, while using a women's business association as a cover for unlicensed activities.

(d)   Dealing with gender-related problems: Many of the women entrepreneurs who have become successful make sure that they are open and transparent to their spouses in order to cultivate their trust and co-operation. Some run the business independently from the husband to minimize his influence. Others focus their time and effort on one (or a few businesses) in order to be able to develop it while still taking care of their family.

1. Introduction

1.1 Background and Objectives

The importance of the economic contribution of micro and small enterprises (MSEs) along with women's participation in the MSE sector has increased tremendously since the mid-1980s. Indeed, the MSEs (herein defined as enterprises employing between 1 and 49 persons) have now become the main source of employment and incomes for the majority of people in developing countries, including Tanzania. Moreover, participation in the MSE sector is widely seen by policy-makers as well as donors as a means of economically empowering marginalized groups, including women (Hanna-Andersson, 1995).

Increased participation of women in the MSE sector has not only improved their access to independent cash income and their control over economic resources, but also posed a socio-cultural challenge (Koda, 1995; Mbughuni, 1994). For example, women are increasingly contributing to meeting household economic needs, a role that was traditionally left to men in many societies. However, women's involvement in business can also represent an additional responsibility on top of the multiple roles that they have traditionally played in society.

A number of initiatives have been taken by governments, donors and Non-Government Organizations (NGOs), both local and international, to increase the start-up rates and performance of women-owned MSEs in Tanzania. Nevertheless, women in the sector are still found predominantly in low-growth areas earning lower revenues than their male counterparts (Rutashobya, 1995). For many women, their involvement in business activities has yet to bring them to a point of economic sustainability and advance them in a manner that is beneficial to them and to the economy in general. In particular, the limited performance of women-owned enterprises may not have enabled them to create meaningful and sustainable enterprises that are able to withstand the challenges posed by globalization.

It is against this background that the International Labour Organization's (ILO) InFocus Programme on Boosting Employment through Small Enterprise Development (IFP/SEED) commissioned a study to highlight the factors affecting women entrepreneurs in creating meaningful and sustainable jobs in Tanzania, Zambia and Ethiopia. The work has been supported by the ILO–Ireland Aid Partnership Programme, with reference to the IFP/SEED team working on Women's Entrepreneurship Development and Gender Equality (WEDGE). The University of Dar es Salaam Entrepreneurship Centre (UDEC) was commissioned to carry out the research in Tanzania.

The research programme was divided into two phases. The first phase entailed identifying and documenting the needs and major issues hampering the performance of women in MSEs. This was done through secondary research on women entrepreneurs and their experiences. The output of the first phase was a review of what is already known about women entrepreneurs and their experiences, and it also highlighted critical issues that needed to be explored in further field research. The second phase of the research entailed an empirical study of women's experiences in developing MSEs. This document presents the detailed findings from the field research conducted with 128 women entrepreneurs in Tanzania. In order to put the two-stage research in perspective, a summary of the secondary research findings is presented below, followed by the problem statement, definitions and methodology used in the field study. The research findings are presented in Chapters 2 to 5. The team of national consultants, UDEC, prepared their conclusions from the field research, as well as a set of proposals for support interventions, and these are presented in Chapter 6.

The final part of the ILO-driven research process in Tanzania involved bringing the findings, conclusions and proposed interventions to a National Symposium on Women's Entrepreneurship, held at Sea Cliff Hotel, Dar es Salaam, on 22 November 2002. The second half of this symposium involved a participatory consultative process in which four working groups were created to review various clusters of proposed interventions. The outcome of the working groups' deliberations was a final set of recommendations, as presented in Chapter 7. These recommendations serve to inform the ongoing work of the ILO's IFP/SEED programme and its team engaged on Women's Entrepreneurship Development and Gender Equality (WEDGE) in Tanzania. They also form the basis of the Action Programme prepared between the ILO and the Ministry of Industry and Trade SME Section.

1.2   Major Factors Hampering the Performance of Women Entrepreneurs

The secondary research concluded that women in the MSE sector are concentrated in the informal, micro, low growth, low profit areas, where competition is intense. These include food vending, tailoring, batik making, beauty salons, decorations, local brewing, catering, pottery, basket making, food processing and charcoal selling. The main reasons are that these sectors require relatively small start-up capital and are thus easy to enter. The incidence of growth of their MSEs is very low, and indeed much lower than that of male-owned enterprises. The secondary research also identified the main constraints to performance of women-owned enterprises at micro, meso and macro levels.

At the micro level, the main issues are the women entrepreneurs' limited education, skills and business experience. At the meso level, the main constraints are limited access to support services, including loan levels suited to their business needs, technical and management training, advice and marketing. These problems arise from the limited capacity and outreach of existing institutions as well as the women entrepreneur's inability to afford to pay for the services. In the case of micro-finance, the problem is mainly limited to lack of access to substantial loans. To some extent, micro-credit is now widely available, especially in urban areas, thanks to donor support and the popular solidarity group-lending model. Another problem is that women's advocacy organizations appear to be weak, making it hard for women to have their voices heard. Also, the laws and regulations affecting businesses (including licensing procedures) were designed for relatively large business activities and are therefore difficult for microenterprises to comply with – and these are predominantly owned by women. Corruption and bureaucracy make matters worse especially for women, who are more vulnerable to physical pressure from corrupt officials.

At the broader macro environment level, the main barrier to the performance of women-owned enterprises is a cultural environment that makes it more difficult for women to start and run enterprises due to their perceptions about traditional reproductive roles. Women are obliged to divide their time between their family and community roles and running the business.

By and large, existing literature on women in the MSE sector has focused mainly on those women operating informal microenterprises, and it tends to generalize the issues and problems to all MSEs. In reality, the incidence and impact of these constraints may vary significantly from one size category of the MSE sector to another. No systematic research has been done to capture these differences, in particular with regard to women involved in growing and expanding MSEs.

1.3   Research Problem and Objectives

The secondary research concludes that only a very small proportion of women entrepreneurs manage to develop small businesses. Perhaps this is not surprising in light of the multitude of barriers that they face. Yet, there is little information as to how the few women who do develop their enterprises from informal activities at the micro level to small and medium enterprises manage to do so in the face of this very difficult environment. A lot can be learned from the experiences of these women.

The overall objective of this primary phase of the study was therefore to understand the processes and critical factors for women involved in formalising their enterprises or developing small enterprises.

The empirical study attempted to answer the following questions:
- To what extent do women entrepreneurs aspire, try to and actually achieve growth?[1] This entailed determining the extent to which women who start microenterprises:
    o Aspire to grow, or formalize their businesses;
    o Have attempted to grow;
    o Have actually developed from micro to small or formalized enterprises and;
    o Are constrained to grow or formalize.
- What strategies are adopted by those women entrepreneurs who manage to formalize their businesses, and by those who develop from one level to the other?
- What role, if any, does the support environment play in facilitating upward mobility of women entrepreneurs?

---

[1] In this study, we are interested in "growth" as measured by traditional economic criteria. This does not mean that non-economic criteria (especially as seen from the MSE operator) are unimportant. It should also be noted that we do not start with an indication of how much growth we are looking for. One of the objectives of this study is to explore the extent to which growth occurs among women-owned MSEs. We use a combination of indicators to establish this.

1.4   Definitions and Interpretations

For the purpose of common understanding, this study defined microenterprises as those enterprises employing between 1- 9 employees and small enterprises as being those enterprises employing between 10 – 49 employees. Women's enterprises are those which were started, are owned and are managed by women. This means the woman is both the major owner and decision-maker of the enterprise. This definition was necessary in order to exclude those women who run businesses started by or owned by men. This definition is in line with the need to empower women in terms of ensuring they have greater access to and control over resources and decision-making. Upward mobility was measured by a combination of indicators, including increased number of employees, formalization, quality of employment, improvements in premises used, and other businesses established.

1.5   Research Methodology

1.5.1 Research design

The study comprised a sample survey of 128 women entrepreneurs, followed by an in-depth study of a smaller group of 15 women, all drawn from the 128. The study focused on women in three women dominated activities: food processing, textile, and beauty services in three urban centres: Arusha, Dar es Salaam and Zanzibar. These are amongst the main commercial centres of Tanzania. Zanzibar was selected because of its cultural difference from Tanzania mainland. While Christians dominate Tanzania mainland, Moslems dominate Zanzibar. Germans and British ruled Tanzania mainland while Zanzibar was ruled by Arabs from Oman and the British. Since we were interested in upward mobility, only women who had been in business for at least two years were included. This is because those who have not been in business for that long are unlikely to have had enough experiences in trying to develop their enterprises.

1.5.2 Survey sample and sampling procedure

Generally, there is no reliable list of micro and small enterprises (MSEs) from which a sampling frame could be drawn. The first step was to develop a list of potential respondents. This was drawn from business associations including Tanzania Chamber of Commerce, Industry and Agriculture (TCCIA), Federation of Associations of Women Entrepreneurs in Tanzania (FAWETA) and Tanzania Food Processors' Association (TAFOPA).   Lists provided by the National Bureau of Statistics (NBS); business development services (BDS) providers and other records available at the University of Dar es Salaam Entrepreneurship Centre (UDEC) were also used.

From the list, respondents were selected according to the number required in each geographical area and for each sector and size category. However, most of these sources of data were not reliable, up-to-date, and complete. In some cases the list did not show the number of years the women had been in business, which was a key selection criteria. In many instances the sources did not show the number of employees in the business. It was quite challenging to locate the women entrepreneurs given that

4

most of the lists did not show their exact location. During the actual selection of the women entrepreneurs, similar available respondents replaced missing cases. An additional strategy in locating the women entrepreneurs was snowballing, i.e. by asking respondents to identify other women they knew had been in business for at least two years in the selected sectors.

The actual number of respondents from each region, by sector and by size is as shown in Table 1.1.

Table 1.1: Number of Respondents from Each Region, by Sector and by Size

Size	Sector	Dar es Salaam		Arusha		Zanzibar		Total	
		Number	%	Number	%	Number	%	Number	%
Micro	Textile	22	24.7	9	10.1	5	5.6	36	40.4
	Health and Beauty	12	13.5	9	10.1	6	6.7	27	30.3
	Food processing	14	15.7	7	7.9	5	5.6	26	29.2
	Total	**48**	**53.9**	**25**	**28.1**	**16**	**18.0**	**89**	**100**
Small	Textile	8	20.5	8	20.5	4	10.3	20	51.3
	Food processing	6	15.4	3	7.7	4	10.3	13	33.3
	Health and Beauty	3	7.7	3	7.7	-	-	6	15.4
	Total	**17**	**43.6**	**14**	**35.9**	**8**	**20.5**	**39**	**100**
Total		**65**	**50.8**	**39**	**30.5**	**24**	**18.7**	**128**	**100**

Women entrepreneurs in food processing were engaged in processing, packing and selling grains, baby foods, jams, honey, meat, juices, wines, butter, etc. Those in textile were engaged in custom tailoring for shorts and dresses, making wedding dresses, batik making, manufacture of bags, dolls, etc. Those in health and beauty were engaged in hair dressing, hair plaiting, manicure, massage, dressing of brides, etc.

The locational distribution of the respondents mirrors the statistical distribution of MSEs in Tanzania. Although data on regional distribution of enterprises are not available, it is known that a majority of enterprises are in Dar es Salaam. Over three-quarters of tax collected in the country comes from Dar es Salaam. About two-thirds of the sample is made of microenterprises, reflecting the skewed distribution of MSEs in favour of microenterprises. The distribution reflects gender differences by size category; women are under-represented in the small and over-represented in the micro-enterprise category.

1.5.3 Data collection procedures and analysis

A semi-structured questionnaire (Annex 1) was used to elicit information on the profile of the respondent and her business; motives for starting the business; developments in the business since it started; future plans and growth motivation; critical barriers to growth; perceived opportunities and barriers for realising them; role of support services and institutions in facilitating/hindering performance, and willingness to partake in a more detailed in-depth interview. To capture growth, respondents were asked about their sales, workforce and investment levels when the business started and at the present time. However, it was found that the responses to questions on sales and investments were inconsistent and hence there is limited significant reporting on quantitative sales and investment figures. Open-ended questions in the questionnaire made it possible to capture qualitative information as well.

Three researchers and three research assistants[2] were involved in data collection. The research assistants were oriented to the study objectives and processes through a one-day workshop held in Dar es Salaam prior to data collection. The researchers and research assistants started data collection in Dar es Salaam together. This gave them the opportunity to share experiences and make any necessary adjustments to the interview process and the questionnaire. After that, each researcher proceeded to one of the regions to collect data with an assistant. Given the unique culture of Zanzibar, a Moslem female research assistant from Zanzibar was assigned to data collection in the island. Before the in-depth study started, the survey data was processed and analysed in order to select the women to be covered in the in-depth study and identify issues that needed to be clarified through the more intensive interviews.

1.5.4 The In-depth Study

The objectives of the in-depth study were to get personal experiences of the women and their attempts, successes and failures in becoming upwardly mobile. During the survey, a total of 15 women entrepreneurs were selected (from the 128 who responded to the survey) for a more in-depth study to better understand their experiences in developing MSEs. The focus was on experiences and facilitating and constraining factors, as well as strategies that they used to develop their enterprises. The women entrepreneurs were selected on the basis of what they had reported in the survey. The composition of the women studied was designed to make it possible to learn from different types of experiences and to make comparisons. One group had a mixture of women who had experienced upward mobility, those who had experienced some growth, and those who had not experienced upward mobility. The businesses included as the basis for selection were therefore in food processing, beauty or tailoring activities. However, some of the women operate other business activities as well. The criterion given in Table 1.2 was used to select those women to be studied in-depth from the sample survey.

---

[2] Initially, it was planned that two research assistants would be required. However, it was later learnt that access to women entrepreneurs in Zanzibar would be more assured if a Zanzibar woman was used as a research assistant.

Table 1.2: Basis for Selection of Respondents for In-Depth Study

No Significant Upward mobility:	Some Upward mobility:	Significant Upward mobility:
No increase or an increase of less than 3 employees	An increase of 3-5 employees	An increase of more than 6 employees, and a change from micro to small
Nana (tailor-DSM) Nestoria (beautician-DSM) Naomi (FP-Arusha) Narcia (FP-Arusha)	Modesta (tailor-DSM) Martina (tailor (DSM) Meriana (FP-DSM) Margareth (tailor-DSM) Meritta (beautician-Arusha) Matilda (bagmaker-DSM) Matrona (beautician-DSM)	Upendo (tailor-DSM) Urbania (tailor-DSM) Ulkaria (beautician-Arusha) Ukweli (Food Processor-DSM)

FP = Food Processor

The names used in this report are fictitious and have been chosen to make the reader aware of the extent to which the woman entrepreneurs being referred to have achieved upward mobility. As can be seen in Table 1.2 above, women whose names start with "N" have not achieved significant upward mobility. Names starting with "M" refer to women who have achieved some (moderate) upward mobility, while those with names starting with "U" have achieved significant upward mobility.

An interview guide (Annex 2) was used to guide data collection in the in-depth interviews. However, during the interviews, follow-up (probing) questions were asked as and when necessary. Questions were replicated and responses crosschecked with those of other respondents.

Analysis was done by tracking common themes, experiences and evidence on strategies, approaches, processes, opportunities, barriers, etc., which have facilitated or hindered women's upward mobility. Data analysis was a continuous process, where the researchers periodically convened to discuss and share observations and issues to be probed further. Experiences of each of the 15 women entrepreneurs were summarized by theme or issue in templates to facilitate cross-case analysis. In this report, the findings of the in-depth analysis are integrated with the field survey results.

2. Profile of the Women Entrepreneurs and their Enterprises

In order to put the results of the study in perspective, the profile of the women and their enterprises is presented by age, level of education, marital status, experience, family background, number of children and type of family, age of the business, number of employees, types of enterprises, and number of businesses currently operating.

2.1 Profile of the Women Entrepreneurs in the Survey

2.1.1 Age

As shown on Table 2.1, a large proportion (40.6 per cent) of the women surveyed were aged between 31 and 40 years. Indeed over 70 per cent of respondents were aged between 31 and 50 years. When the age analysis is done by region, the distribution is the same. However, Zanzibar has the highest proportion of older entrepreneurs. While women in textile and food processing were aged between 31 and 50, entrepreneurs in beauty care were found to be younger. Over 80 per cent were aged between 20 – 40 years (see Annex 3.1). This could be explained by the nature of this industry as young women may be more attracted to beauty care. Indeed, many younger women indicated that it was their hobby to make other women beautiful.

Table 2.1: Age of the Women Entrepreneurs

Age Group	Dar es Salaam		Arusha		Zanzibar		Total	
	Number	%	Number	%	Number	%	Number	%
Below 20	1	1.5	-	-	-	-	1	0.8
20-30 years	16	24.6	6	15.4	4	16.7	26	20.3
31-40 years	25	38.5	17	43.6	10	41.7	52	40.6
41-50 years	18	27.7	15	38.5	6	25.0	39	30.5
Over 50 years	5	6.1	1	2.6	4	16.7	5	7.0
Non-response	1	1.5	-	-	-	-	1	0.8
Total	65	100	39	100	24	100	128	100.0

The results also show that only a tiny proportion was below 20 or over 50 years old. This might be explained by the fact that older women may have grown up in a cultural context (pre-liberalization) where there was little encouragement to do business and hence were less inclined to start business even in their later life when it is more common for women to do so.

2.1.2 Level of education

Previous studies show that generally, women entrepreneurs have low levels of education. The results of this study however show that, about a third of the women entrepreneurs in the sample have only primary education, while the majority have completed at least secondary education ('O' Level and above), with over a quarter having post-secondary education (Table 2.2).

One of the reasons why these results are different is that previous studies in the MSE sector focused more on informal sector activities where the majority of women MSE operators are to be found. This study deliberately sought to include enterprises which are formally established. It is likely that educated women are more likely to develop formal businesses. Also, some women with secondary or higher education tend to stay away from the dominant informal sector economic activities such as food vending, basketry, charcoal retailing, local brewing, etc.

Table 2.2: Women Entrepreneurs' Level of Education

	Dar es Salaam		Arusha		Zanzibar		Total	
	Number	%	Number	%	Number	%	Number	%
Never attended	-	-	-	-	1	4.2	1	0.8
Primary school	20	30.8	5	12.8	10	41.7	35	27.3
O-Level Secondary	22	33.8	17	43.6	10	41.7	49	38.3
A-Level Secondary	4	6.2	3	7.7	-	-	7	5.5
Post-secondary certificate	10	15.4	7	17.9	1	4.2	18	14.1
Ordinary Diploma	7	10.8	6	15.4	2	8.3	15	11.7
Advanced Diploma/Degree	1	1.5	-	-	-	-	1	0.8
No response	1	1.5	1	2.6	-	-	2	1.6
Total	**65**	**100**	**39**	**100**	**24**	**100**	**128**	**100.0**

Women entrepreneurs in the beauty sector were found to have relatively higher education compared to the other sectors (see Annex 3.1). Over 90 per cent had secondary education or above, compared to 65 per cent for textile and 70 per cent for food processing. While Zanzibar has the highest proportion (46 per cent) of women entrepreneurs with primary or low education, Arusha has the highest proportion (over 85 per cent) of those with at least secondary school education.

2.1.3 Experience prior to start-up

Before starting their current businesses, most (53 per cent) of the women entrepreneurs were employees. As Table 2.3 shows, about a fifth were running other businesses, while 12.5 per cent came straight from school. Most of the women (73.4 per cent) had either previous employment experience or experience in running another business before starting the current one.

Table 2.3 Women Entrepreneurs' Previous Experiences

	Dar es Salaam		Arusha		Zanzibar		Total	
	Number	%	Number	%	Number	%	Number	%
Employed	34	52.3	28	71.8	7	29.2	69	53.9
In another business	11	16.9	5	12.8	9	37.5	25	19.5
Student	10	15.4	2	5.1	4	16.7	16	12.5
Housewife	6	9.2	1	2.6	3	12.5	10	7.8
Unemployed	4	6.2	2	5.1	1	4.2	7	5.5
Non response	-	-	1	2.6	-	-	1	0.8
Total	**65**	**100.0**	**39**	**100.0**	**24**	**100.0**	**128**	**100.0**

This finding is inconsistent with the literature on Tanzanian MSEs, which shows that women entrepreneurs have limited employment experience. The fact that many women entrepreneurs were previously employed could be a reflection of their higher levels of education. Sector-wise, food processing was found to have a very high proportion (over 90 per cent) of women entrepreneurs who were previously employed or who had owned another business. A large proportion of women entrepreneurs in Arusha was also found to have had employment experience compared to other regions. This may reflect their higher levels of education relative to the other regions. Consistent with earlier research, most women were previously employed in traditionally female occupations such as nursing, teaching, secretarial and other clerical works (Table 2.4).

Table 2.4   Types of Employment Experience

Experience	Number	%
Secretary	19	14.8
SME employees	10	7.8
Clerical	9	7.0
Accountant	7	5.5
Nurse	7	5.5
Managerial	5	3.9
Supervisory	5	3.9
Teacher	5	3.9
Others	5	3.9
None	56	43.8
Total	**128**	**100**

2.1.4   Marital status

Most of the women entrepreneurs started their business activity after getting married. This is reflected in Table 2.5, which shows that about 70 per cent of the respondents were married before starting the business and have remained so until now. Four women have become separated and two divorced after starting their business.

Table 2.5   Marital Status Prior to Starting the Business and Currently

Marital Status	Before Starting Business		Now	
	Number	%	Number	%
Married	89	69.5	87	68.0
Single	31	24.2	24	18.8
Divorced	4	3.1	6	4.7
Separated	1	0.8	5	3.9
Widowed	2	1.6	4	3.1
No response	1	0.8	2	1.6
Total	**128**	**100.0**	**128**	**100.0**

2.1.5 Family background

Family background tends to influence one's access to resources and life experience, as well as to networks. Table 2.6 below analyses the educational level of the women's spouses and parents. More details can be found in Annex 3.2.

About 42 per cent of the women's spouses have diploma or higher education, whereas slightly over 85 per cent had at least secondary education. This shows that the women entrepreneurs are mainly married to people with relatively high levels of education. Compared to Dar es Salaam and Arusha, however the proportion of spouses who have attained high levels of education (Ordinary Diploma and above) is lower in Zanzibar (13 per cent compared to 40 per cent and 38 per cent for Dar es Salaam and Arusha respectively).

By contrast, the majority of the women's parents have primary education or lower. About a third of their mothers have never received a formal education, while only 3.1 per cent have mothers with diploma or higher. The corresponding proportion for fathers is 10 per cent. A similar trend is shown when the analysis is done at regional level. Comparatively, however, the proportions of women entrepreneur's fathers and mothers who never attended school is much higher in Zanzibar (37 per cent and 67 per cent respectively) compared to Dar es Salaam (6 per cent and 23 per cent) and Arusha (18 per cent and 21 per cent). Likewise the difference in education level between fathers and mothers is much more pronounced in Zanzibar where only 37 per cent of fathers had never attended school compared to 67 per cent of mothers.

Table 2.6 Family Educational Background

Education Level	Spouse		Father		Mother	
	Number	%	Number	%	Number	%
Never been to school	2	1.6	20	15.6	39	30.5
Primary school	9	7.0	48	37.5	54	42.2
O-Level secondary school	37	28.9	15	11.7	14	10.9
A-Level secondary school	2	1.6	1	0.8	-	-
Post secondary certificate	9	7.0	6	4.7	-	-
Ordinary diploma	12	9.4	4	3.1	4	3.1
Advanced diploma/First Degree	16	12.5	6	4.7	-	-
Postgraduate Qualification	16	12.5	2	1.6	-	-
Standard 8	-	-	17	13.3	11	8.6
Not applicable	18	14.1	5	3.9	3	2.3
No response	7	5.5	4	3.1	3	2.3
Total	**128**	**100.0**	**128**	**100.0**	**128**	**100.0**

Another important observation is that women entrepreneurs in Dar es Salaam have relatively more educated parents than in Arusha and Zanzibar. Out of the fathers with high education (diploma or above), 66 per cent come from Dar es Salaam. One possible explanation could be the effect of migration, as there is a historical migration of the educated to Dar es Salaam in search of career opportunities. The level of education of fathers in Dar es Salaam could also be a reflection of their occupations (over 33 per cent were professional employees or managers).

The results also reflect the historical marginalization of women in terms of their access to education. Generally, the entrepreneurs' fathers have higher levels of educational attainment compared to their mothers.

In terms of professional background, the analysis in Table 2.7 reveals that more than 84 per cent of the women surveyed had husbands who were managers, entrepreneurs or professionals. One third had spouses who were themselves entrepreneurs. Although data on distribution of the male population by occupations is unavailable, it is likely that the respondents' husbands are over-represented in the professional and managerial occupations. This means that potentially they are likely to have better access to financial resources and advice compared to the average women entrepreneur.

Over 60 per cent of spouses with either managerial position or professional employees come from Dar es Salaam, compared to 21 per cent for Arusha and 17 per cent for Zanzibar. Possible reasons could be the higher levels of education attained by spouses in Dar es Salaam.

Interestingly, more than 50 per cent of spouses who are entrepreneurs come from Arusha. Indeed the analysis reveals that women entrepreneurs in Arusha have a relatively high proportion of parents (both mother and father) who are entrepreneurs as compared to Dar es Salaam and Zanzibar. Although data on ethnicity is not available, this finding is not surprising as there is consensus in the entrepreneurship literature in Tanzania that the Chagga people from Kilimanjaro (who also dominate Arusha urban, due to its vicinity to Kilimanjaro) are more likely to start a business.

Table 2.7 Women Entrepreneurs' Family Occupational Background

Occupation of the family	Spouse		Father		Mother	
	Number	%	Number	%	Number	%
Managerial Position	17	13.3	7	5.5	1	0.8
Entrepreneur	35	27.3	34	26.6	23	18.0
Professional Employee	35	27.3	27	21.1	7	5.5
Peasant/Fisherman	1	0.8	31	24.2	22	17.2
Technical Position	2	1.6	7	5.5	-	-
Service/Support employee	13	10.2	14	10.9	4	3.1
Housewife	-	-	-	-	68	53.1
Not applicable	25	19.5	8	6.3	3	2.3
Total	**128**	**100.0**	**128**	**100.0**	**128**	**100.0**

At least half of the respondents came from families where the father is a professional, an entrepreneur or a manager. However, over half of the respondents came from families where the mother was a housewife. Also, 18 per cent of the respondents have mothers who were themselves entrepreneurs. This partly challenges the accepted view that business ownership is a relatively new thing among women entrepreneurs.

Women are said to be constrained partly by their reproductive roles, including taking care of children. A large majority (85.1 per cent) of the women in the sample had children, most of them (57 per cent) had more than two children, and 27 per cent had more than four children (Table 2.8).

Table 2.8 Women Entrepreneurs' Number of Children

Number of children	Dar es Salaam		Arusha		Zanzibar		Total	
	Number	%	Number	%	Number	%	Number	%
None	1	.8	1	0.8	-	-	2	1.6
One	7	5.5	4	3.1	1	0.8	12	9.4
Two	12	9.4	8	6.3	4	3.1	24	18.8
Three	10	7.8	12	9.4	3	2.3	25	19.5
Four	7	5.5	5	3.9	1	0.8	13	10.2
More than four	17	13.3	5	3.9	13	10.2	35	27.0
Not applicable	11	8.6	4	3.1	2	1.6	17	13.3
Total	**65**	**50.8**	**39**	**30.5**	**24**	**18.8**	**128**	**100.0**

A comparison of the number of children by region, reveals that out of the 27.3 per cent of women entrepreneurs who have more than four children, most come from Dar es Salaam (13.3 per cent) and Zanzibar (10.2 per cent). More than 50 per cent of women entrepreneurs in Zanzibar had over 4 children, compared to 26 per cent and 13 per cent for Dar es Salaam and Arusha respectively.

Over half (54 per cent) of the women entrepreneurs in this study had extended families (see Annex 3.3). However, only 31 per cent of women entrepreneurs in Zanzibar have extended families compared to about 60 per cent for Dar es Salaam and Arusha. This could partly be explained by the fact that women entrepreneurs in Zanzibar have a large number of their own children and some are divorced, and therefore they might be reluctant to take on additional people in their families.

The results show that women entrepreneurs had substantial responsibilities, combining business activity with childcare. As indicated above, most live in extended families (Table 2.9). While the extended family implies an additional burden to women entrepreneurs, it could also be a source of labour (paid or unpaid) both at home and in the business.

Table 2.9 Women Entrepreneurs' Type of Family

Type of Family	Food processing		Health and Beauty		Textile		Total	
	Number	%	Number	%	Number	%	Number	%
Extended family	21	53.5	15	45.5	34	60.7	70	54.4
Nuclear family	7	18	7	21.2	13	23.2	27	21.1
Mother and children	10	25.6	2	6	5	8.9	17	13.3
Alone	-	-	7	21.2	3	5.4	10	8
Living with parents/relative	1	2.9	-	-	1	1.8	2	1.6
Non-response	-	-	2	6.1	-	-	2	1.6
Total	**39**	**100**	**33**	**100**	**56**	**100**	**128**	**100**

In summary, the sample of women interviewed in this study are clearly not typical of the women entrepreneurs described in other literature. Nor would they be, because the fieldwork for this study focussed on women in formal, growing businesses – and they are not the norm in Tanzania. The literature generally shows that Tanzanian women entrepreneurs have low levels of education and very limited access to economic resources. The women in this study however have relatively high levels of education and experience, with parents and/or spouses who are relatively well to do.

2.1.6 General Profile of the Women Entrepreneurs who participated in the In-Depth Study

Of the 15 women who participated in the in-depth study, most (9) have micro businesses, and the rest have businesses employing between 10 and 21 persons. Also, 11 are married, 2 single, one separated, and one widowed. Age-wise, 3 of the women are in their 20s, 7 in their 30s, 5 in their 40s and 1 in her 50s. The women came from a variety of backgrounds. In terms of education, almost all completed secondary school. Only three (Nestoria, Ulkaria and Nana) have had no employment experience. Two of these (Nana and Nestoria) are the only ones who do not have secondary education. Interestingly six of them were trained and employed as secretaries. Another three worked as clerks or telephone operators (Martina, Matilda and Urbania). Those who had been employed acknowledged that the employment experience has been invaluable in business by providing networks (including their first customers) and instilling confidence to deal with different types of people and situations. Naomi is the only diploma holder, while Modesta is the only degree holder. The women's family backgrounds range from entrepreneurs and managers to peasants.

Some of the women had been socialized to business activity at an early age by either actually doing business or acquiring the relevant skills. Margareth, a successful tailor, sold ice cream to other children when she was in primary school to raise pocket money. Matrona, a successful beautician, started a poultry farm when she was in Form Three. Modesta's father was a tailor. This inspired Modesta and gave her the opportunity to start playing with the sewing machine from when she was in primary school. Urbania, the most upwardly mobile of the women, had a similar experience. Her mother had a sewing machine, which she left free for the children to use. While in class six, she was able to make different types of dresses, without any formal training. Meriana, a woman involved in food processing whose main product is peanut butter, reports that her mother used to make the same product.

2.2 Profile of the Women's Enterprises

2.2.1 Age of the Enterprises

About three-quarters of the businesses were established between 1995 and 2000, meaning that they are between §two and seven years old, and 7 per cent were established before 1985, when the first steps were taken to liberalize the economy (Table 2.10).

Table 2.10 Year of Establishment by Sector

Year	Dar es Salaam		Arusha		Zanzibar		Total	
	Number	%	Number	%	Number	%	Number	%
Before 1985	1	1.5	2	5.1	6	25.0	9	7.0
1986-1994	11	16.9	8	20.5	5	20.8	24	18.8
1995-1999	33	50.8	25	64.1	12	50.0	70	54.7
2000	18	27.7	4	10.3	1	4.2	23	18.0
No Response	2	3.1	-	-	-	-	2	1.6
Total	**65**	**100.0**	**39**	**100.0**	**24**	**100.0**	**128**	**100.0**

Analysis of the age of enterprises by sector and region reveals interesting findings. Probably as a reflection of young age of women entrepreneurs in the health and beauty sector, over 80 per cent of business were established between 1995 and 2000; the proportions for food processing and textiles are 69 per cent and 66 per cent respectively (Annex 3.4).

Moreover, of the 9 oldest firms studied, 5 are in food processing (4 of which are in Zanzibar). Also 6 of the oldest firms are in Zanzibar. This could imply that of the three sectors under study, more food processing firms from Zanzibar were established prior to 1985. This could also be a reflection of the older age of women entrepreneurs in Zanzibar. (It should be recalled that 42 per cent of women entrepreneurs in Zanzibar were over 41 years old.)

2.2.2 Number of employees

The 128 women entrepreneurs who participated in the survey have created a total of 752 paid jobs (including their own jobs) in the businesses covered in detail by the survey (see table 2.11 below), and 231 paid jobs in other businesses[3], making a total of 983 jobs or an average of 9.7 jobs per woman entrepreneur.   In addition, the 128 women engage 83 apprentices and 28 unpaid family members.   The additional jobs created in the women entrepreneurs' other businesses, as well as the work and training provided to apprentices and unpaid family members, constitute significant contributions to employment creation and economic development.

Table 2.11 Number of Employees

Type of Employment Created	Number of Employees		
	Male	Female	Total
Full-time employees	186	361	547
Part-time/casual employees	68	90	158
Paid family members	18	29	47
Total Paid workers	**272**	**480**	**752**

Table 2.12 shows that the majority of the enterprises (67 per cent) in the survey employ between 1 and 9 employees. Although this study defined small enterprises as those

---

[3] Several of the women entrepreneurs had established more than one business, although the study concentrated on findings from their main business activity.

employing between 1 and 49, only 6 of the respondents had over 20 employees. The pattern is the same for all regions and sectors (see Annex 3.5 for details).

Table 2.12   Number of Workers (Including the owner)

	Dar es Salaam		Arusha		Zanzibar		Total N	
	Number	%	Number	%	Number	%	Number	%
1-5	34	52.3	16	41	14	59	64	50
6-9	14	21.5	6	15.4	2	8	22	17.2
10-20	14	21.5	11	28.2	8	33	33	25.8
Over 20	3	4.6	3	7.7	-	-	6	4.7
Non-response	-	-	3	7.7	-	-	3	2.3
Total	**65**	**100**	**39**	**100**	**24**	**100**	**128**	**100**

2.2.3   Type of Business Licence

Over 70 per cent of respondents had some form of a business licence (Table 2.13). While 38 per cent had minor licences[4], about 40 per cent had principal licences. Only about 23 per cent of women entrepreneurs in this study had no business licence.

Table 2.13   Type of Business Licence Held

	Food Processing		Health and Beauty		Textile		Total	
	Number	%	Number	%	Number	%	Number	%
Principal license	10	7.8	17	13.3	23	18.0	50	39.1
Minor license	12	9.4	12	9.4	25	19.5	49	38.3
No license	17	13.3	4	3.1	8	6.3	29	22.7
Total	**39**	**30.5**	**33**	**25.8**	**56**	**43.8**	**128**	**100.0**

When the analysis is done by sector, over 50 per cent of those who don't have any business licences are in food processing. Indeed over 40 per cent of respondents in this sector did not have any licence compared to 23 per cent for the entire sample. This is partly explained by the stringent licensing requirements for food processing activities. Over 85 per cent of firms in the both textile and health and beauty sectors had either a minor or a principal licence.

2.2.4   Legal status of businesses

Over 88 per cent of the businesses in this study are organized as sole proprietorships. Only two firms are limited liability companies, while 9.4 per cent are partnerships. There is no noticeable difference in legal status by region or sectors. However, both limited companies are in food processing and are located in Arusha. This is consistent with the observation that women entrepreneurs in Arusha have higher levels of education and are likely to have better access to resources in terms of well-to-do husbands.

---

[4] A business with a minor licence can be described as semi-formal. A minor licence is a permit issued to enterprises, which are too small to justify the fees normally charged for a regular (principal) licence. Minor licences are regulated and issued by local authorities, while a principal licence is a formal licence regulated by some piece of national legislation. It attracts a relatively large annual fee and the licencee is also liable to income tax.

Table 2.14 Legal Status of Businesses

Legal Status	Food processing		Health and Beauty		Textile		Total	
	Number	%	Number	%	Number	%	Number	%
Sole proprietorship	33	25.8	31	24.2	49	38.3	113	88.3
Partnership	4	3.1	2	1.6	6	4.7	12	9.4
Limited liability company	2	1.6	-	-	-	-	2	1.6
Non-response	-	-	-	-	1	0.8	1	0.8
Total	**39**	**30.5**	**33**	**25.8**	**56**	**43.8**	**128**	**100.0**

3.   The Process of Starting and Developing the Businesses

3.1   Motivation for Starting Business

During the field survey, respondents were asked to state up to three main reasons for going into business. The motives vary from one woman to another, as well as from one business to another for the same woman. The reasons cited during the survey are as summarized in Table 3.1. The most common motive for going into business was to create employment for the woman herself. Other motives include supplementing income, enjoyment of work, use of existing skills and competencies, as well as doing business as a hobby (personal interest). Analysis of the start-up motives by sector reveal no major differences.

Table 3.1   Motives for Starting the Business

Motivation	Food processing		Health and Beauty		Textile		Total	
	Number	%	Number	%	Number	%	Number	%
Create employment for self	12	9.4	10	7.8	17	13.3	39	30.5
Supplement income	13	10.2	3	2.3	21	16.4	37	28.9
I enjoy doing the work involved	2	1.6	5	3.9	2	1.6	9	7.0
To use skills and competencies I had acquired	2	1.6	3	2.3	3	2.3	8	6.3
Personal interest (hobby)	1	0.8	2	1.6	4	3.1	7	5.5
To have something to have control over	1	0.8	1	0.8	2	1.6	4	3.1
Others	8	6.3	9	7.0	7	5.5	24	18.8
Total	**39**	**30.5**	**33**	**25.8**	**56**	**43.8**	**128**	**100.0**

The in-depth interviews yielded more detailed understanding of the motives for starting businesses. For those women who are married to relatively well-to-do men, the main reasons for starting businesses were to create their own jobs and to reduce dependency on their husbands' income. Married women indicated that it is unwise to rely totally on their spouses' income, because anything can happen to the spouse leading to serious consequences for the family. Narcia, the only woman in the in-depth sample who started business after retirement, was motivated by the need to have a job to keep herself busy, as well as a source of income. Urbania started making dresses for herself and her friends as a hobby and only got involved seriously in business because of the interest shown in her work by her customers. Margareth, a beautician, started business on a part-time basis because she had a hobby in beauty, but also her salary was too small to enable her meet her needs. However, she did not start a business until a woman who had expertise in hair styling approached her and convinced her to start a salon. Modesta, a marketing graduate, started a tailoring business as a temporary activity when she was waiting to take up her next job.

The women are also motivated by the fact that doing business improves their status in society as well as in the family. Urbania says that she now plans with her husband because she is able to make a significant financial contribution in everything they do. She believes that this could not happen if her contribution was mere words. Some of the women started with activities which were meant for producing goods or services for home consumption and just selling the surplus. The thinking behind that was that the woman felt she was able to produce better quality or more conveniently than she could obtain from the market. Ukweli and Naomi started keeping diary cows so that the children could have quality milk. Then later, they decided to set up what they see as "real" businesses. Upendo used to do tailoring activities at home for the children and later gradually started taking orders from outside. Successful women entrepreneurs in Kenya inspired Meritta and Meriana during visits to their family members living there.

As to why women choose the types of activities that they engage in, the in-depth interviews suggest four possible reasons. First, some women start doing certain things because they enjoy doing them. This is the case with most of the women in tailoring and beauty care. When asked whether they would stop the businesses given alternative and better paying jobs, all women, including Nana, who is struggling to make ends meet, categorically indicated that whatever they earn elsewhere, they would still maintain the businesses on the side. They see the businesses as important parts of their lives and not just mechanisms for generating income. This observation contradicts the view that women in the MSE sector are motivated mainly by economic necessity and "dislike" what they are doing because they are compelled to do so by economic necessity. We should therefore acknowledge that the women entrepreneurs are generally strongly committed to their activities, even if they are still operating at a very small scale.

The second reason is that women have been socialized to do certain kinds of activities from their childhood, and when they choose self-employment, they tend to think of these activities first. Meriana developed an interest in peanut butter making from her mother. After attending a course on processing of different foods, she chose peanut butter making. Almost all the women in tailoring grew up in families where they had the opportunity to observe people using tailoring machines. A third reason is that since many of the women face resource constraints, they start with activities which are easy to establish. Later on, they change to something that they really want to do. Matrona's interest was in a boutique, but since she could not raise the money she needed to start the kind of boutique that she wanted, she decided to start with a salon, which required less resources.

Fourthly, some women chose activities which enable them to effectively combine business with their family responsibilities. Upendo says that one of the reasons why tailoring appealed to her is because she could work from home, while taking care of the children at the same time.

3.2   Start-up Process

While some of the women started formal businesses with licences, most started informally as part-time activities. Of the 15 women who participated in the in-depth study, 9 started operating from home without any licence. Martina started her first tailoring business without any tailoring facilities. She pretended to be a tailor but actually took orders and got the work done by an established tailor at lower cost, pocketing the difference. Urbania started tailoring on a part-time basis, taking orders from work and using a relative's machine. Three of the four women involved in food processing started working from home and they are still operating without licences. Four of the five beauticians started operating from home as well. Two reasons account for the women's tendency to start informally. First of all, many of the businesses in tailoring and beauty sectors, started as extensions of the women's hobbies or to meet their family needs. Since formalization involves using expensive premises and going through a costly licensing procedure, it is natural that it would not be pursued until it became apparent that the women could make money out of their business activities. Secondly, the women tend to start with very limited resources. For the most part, they had to accumulate savings from the informal activity to enable them to set up their business formally.

3.3   Source of Finance at Start-up and Currently

Table 3.2 shows the main sources of finance when the businesses started and at present the current time (Annex 3.6 analyses the data by sector). The analysis shows that a large majority started and are developing their businesses from their own savings. Indeed, reliance on own savings has increased from two-thirds when they started to almost four-fifths of the women at present. The rest of start-up capital has been provided mainly from the spouse and other relatives. Many married women got their start-up finance from their husbands.

Table 3.2   Sources of Finance when the Business Started and Currently

Source of Finance	When the business started % (N= 128) (multiple responses)				Currently % (N= 128) (multiple responses)			
	Dar es Salaam	Arusha	Zanzibar	Total	Dar es Salaam	Arusha	Zanzibar	Total
Own savings	32.8	25.0	9.4	**67.2**	35.2	25.8	18.0	**78.9**
Credit from MFIs	4.7	2.3	1.6	**8.6**	12.5	10.9	1.6	**25.0**
Credit from friends and family	16.4	3.1	1.6	**21.1**	9.4	3.1	-	**12.5**
Credit from bank	1.6	2.3	-	**3.9**	3.1	7.0	-	**10.2**
From private money lenders	-	-	0.8	**0.8**	0.8	0.8	-	**1.6**
Assistance from spouse	15.6	12.5	4.7	**32.8**	0.8	0.8	-	**1.6**

A high proportion of women entrepreneurs in Dar es Salaam and Arusha used their own funds, and benefited from credit from MFIs, friends and family members, and they were also more likely to benefit from assistance from their spouses. Women entrepreneurs in all regions were unlikely to obtain (or seek) credit from private moneylenders. It was also observed that a larger proportion of women entrepreneurs in Dar es Salaam and Arusha received assistance from their spouses. This can be explained by the fact that many of the spouses hold managerial posts or professional positions, thereby being in a better position to support their wives.

The use of credit from banks has increased, especially among women entrepreneurs in Arusha. Also, utilization of credit from MFIs has increased significantly (8.6 per cent at start up to current 25 per cent). Except for Zanzibar where the number of women entrepreneurs utilising MFIs remained the same, the number using MFIs increased in both Dar es Salaam and Arusha.

As a reflection of the increased utilization of other formal sources of financing, the proportion of women entrepreneurs taking credit from friends and family members decreased from 21.1 per cent to 12.5 per cent. There was however no change in this regard among women entrepreneurs in Arusha.

Another observation is that financial assistance from spouses was mainly used to finance start up. Less than 2 per cent of the women are being assisted by their spouses, compared to 32.8 per cent when they started their businesses. Possible reasons could be using alternative sources of finance, fear of losing control of the business, inability to meet higher requirements for finance, or the spouses do not have sufficient funds.

The in-depth interviews with the 15 women entrepreneurs revealed that even those who have spouses who are relatively well to do have struggled successfully to access finance independently. A number of the women started business activity at a very small scale and therefore did not use much money. Ulkaria and Upendo raised their start-up capital from a combination of rotating credit schemes and borrowing from micro-finance institutions. Six of the 15 women (Urbania, Matrona, Martina, Ulkaria, Meriana and Upendo) have tried to access loans from banks. However, only Urbania and Ulkaria were successful, and both got loans for expansion rather than start-up capital.

3.4   Factors Facilitating in Starting Business

Respondents were asked to indicate the factors, which were helpful in starting their business. Skills and competencies acquired prior to starting the business were cited as having played a critical role in facilitating the start-up (Table 3.3). This is especially because all the sectors studied require specialized skills and particular talents. The women received different kinds of non-financial support from various sources, such as advice given by friends and relatives, moral support and encouragement from spouse, friend (including finances) and family members, etc.

Table 3.3 Factors Facilitating Starting Business

Motivation	Food processing		Health and Beauty		Textile		Total	
	Number	%	Number	%	Number	%	Number	%
Skills, competencies and training I had prior	14	10.9	3	2.3	10	7.8	27	21.1
Non-financial support from family and friends	3	2.3	4	3.1	13	10.2	20	15.6
Availability of own capital	4	3.1	6	4.7	6	4.7	16	12.5
Availability of equipment and working tools	2	1.6	3	2.3	10	7.8	15	11.7
Help from husband	6	4.7	3	2.3	4	3.1	13	10.2
Availability of good working place/premise	1	0.8	6	4.7	3	2.3	10	7.8
Financial support	1	0.8	-	-	1	0.8	2	1.6
Others	6	4.7	6	4.7	8	6.3	20	15.6
Non-responses	2	1.6	2	1.6	1	0.8	5	3.9
Total	**39**	**30.5**	**33**	**25.8**	**56**	**43.8**	**128**	**100.0**

The in-depth discussions with the 15 women entrepreneurs supported these results. For the women involved in food processing, the most critical support factors in starting their businesses were the technical training and access to packing materials and quality labels provided from a UNIDO-supported programme.

Except for Nana and Narcia, the rest of the women got support from their spouses, parents or other close relatives in starting the business, and they report that this support played a very significant role in the development of the business. Five of the women who started business while married (Ukweli, Matilda, Ulkaria, Naomi, and Martina) obtained the initial capital from their husbands and have continued receiving their husband's moral support. Interestingly, all the women who have experienced upward mobility reported that a lot of moral and material support comes from family members, and in many cases help came from the husband. In other cases, it came from an aunt, a sister or a parent. Again the results show that family relationships are an important factor for success among women entrepreneurs.

3.5   Constraints Faced in Establishing the Business

Women entrepreneurs in this study faced a number of constraints in starting their businesses. However, as shown in table 3.4 more than a third of the respondents cited access to markets (difficulties with selling due to competition and limited local demand for their products or services) as the main constraint. In addition, about 11 per cent cited lack of capital/ finance as a constraint. Other constraints include licensing regulations, lack of relevant skills and competencies (especially in the beauty and textile sectors), and inconveniences from the customer on payment. All of these were felt most in the textile sector.

Table 3.4 Constraints in Starting the Business

Constraint	Food processing		Health and Beauty		Textile		Total	
	Number	%	Number	%	Number	%	Number	%
Lack of access to market	13	10.2	17	13.3	17	13.3	47	36.7
Lack of capital	7	5.5	2	1.6	5	3.9	14	10.9
Lack of some skills	1	0.8	2	1.6	8	6.3	11	8.6
Licensing regulations	2	1.6	1	0.8	6	4.7	9	7.0
Difficulties in collecting receivables	2	1.6	2	1.6	5	3.9	9	7.0
Lack of working tools	3	2.3	-	-	3	2.3	6	4.7
Others	7	5.5	7	5.5	9	7.0	23	18.0
None Response	4	3.1	2	1.6	3	2.3	9	7.0
Total	**39**	**30.4**	**33**	**25.8**	**56**	**43.8**	**128**	**100.0**

Other problems cited include access to premises, access to raw materials and problems with employees. Sector-wise, the limited access to markets ranked first in all sectors, while lack of capital was cited more by the food processors, followed by the textile businesses.

3.6 Business Diversification

It is often observed that women tend to establish and run a number of businesses concurrently. Table 3.5 shows that about half of the sample had no other businesses, whereas 30 per cent had one other business, and 16 per cent own more than one other business. The detailed type of activities carried out in the other business are diverse, but in most cases they are petty businesses like selling bread, charcoal, small-scale farming, baking cakes and buns, food vending, poultry and diary.

Table 3.5 Number of Other Businesses Concurrently Run

Number of other businesses	Total	
	Number	%
None	69	53.9
One	38	29.7
More than one	21	16.4
Total	**128**	**100**

The experiences of the 15 women entrepreneurs who participated in the in-depth study shed some light on some of the possible reasons for diversification. Almost all the 15 women had more than one business or more than one product within the same business. For example Ukweli runs a food processing business. Some of her product lines include sausages, peanut butter, mango spices, pickle, "mbilimbi" pickle, and honey. She also keeps diary cattle, and runs a farm to produce some of her ingredients.

One of the motives for diversification is to spread risk. The women entrepreneurs realize that their businesses are vulnerable and therefore start something else to hedge against the unexpected. After running a food processing business informally for four years, Narcia decided to start something which is easier to formalize, just in case one day she would be forced to close the informal food processing enterprise. She set up a small tailoring shop in 1997. Although she has not been forced to close down the first business, its performance has deteriorated due to a number of reasons and now she relies on the tailoring business for her subsistence. Martina has been starting new businesses for two reasons. First, she believes she needs to do so to make more money. Secondly, she believes that having more than one business is a way of countering risk. In 1997, thieves broke into her salon and stole everything, and she revived it using resources from the other businesses. To Martina, having four businesses is not a problem since she says that they are adjacent to each other and hence easy to manage, and they are also complementary. For example, when a man is waiting for a friend to be attended at the salon, he can have a drink at the bar or even take an interest in the tailoring market.

Margareth, a beautician who also runs a tailoring business and a household supplies retail store, sees diversification as a way of ensuring a constant flow of income, given that some businesses are seasonal. Modesta, a business graduate, feels that running one business in an expensive city like Dar es Salaam is not enough. She believes that she can make more money by having more, not fewer businesses.

On the other hand, there are those women who think running more than one business can be very difficult. Upendo says that one business is taking a lot of her time and she cannot see how she could manage to run another effectively and still be a mother at home. Urbania has tried to run two new activities but had to stop within six months because they placed so much time pressure on her that the (original) tailoring business suffered. Later however, she successfully set up a salon adjacent to the tailoring business. She has managed the two activities smoothly, since they are close to each other. She is now planning to start a ready-made garment shop. Meritta, who runs a salon and sells shoes and clothes, thinks that the salon needs all her time, and therefore she does not want to run other businesses. In fact she has decided to stop selling the shoes and clothes in order to concentrate on her salon.

In summary, the motives for diversification vary from one woman to another. For some, it is a way of spreading risk. For others, they had insufficient funds to start up their first choice of business and could only do so later. And for others, they recognized the limited potential in their initial business.

3.7   Incidence of Upward Mobility

One of the major objectives of the study was to establish the extent to which women-owned enterprises have formalized and grown their businesses. It was also intended to identify the owner's plans for developing the businesses. These issues are assessed below.

3.7.1 Formalization

Table 3.6 indicates the changes in various aspects of the businesses when they were established and as they are at present. These aspects include legal status, bank accounts and licences.

Table 3.6   Formalization of Business when Established and at Present

Aspect of Formalization	When started		Currently	
	Frequency	%	Frequency	%
Legal Status				
Sole proprietorship	113	88.3	113	88.3
Partnership	12	9.3	12	9.3
Limited liability company	2	1.6	2	1.6
Non response	1	0.8	1	0.8
Total	**128**	**100.0**	**128**	**100.0**
Licence				
Principal licence	34	26.6	50	39.1
Minor licence	56	43.8	49	38.2
No licence	38	29.6	29	22.7
Total	**128**	**100**	**128**	**100**
Type of Bank Account				
Savings	66	51.6	83	64.8
Current	15	11.7	32	25.0
None	47	36.7	13	10.2
Total	**128**	**100.0**	**128**	**100.0**

In terms of legal status, nothing has changed. All businesses started as sole proprietorships and have remained so. In contrast, there have been significant changes in terms of the type of licences used by the women. The proportion of women with no licences at all has decreased from about 30 per cent when they started business to 23 per cent now. A more dramatic change can be observed in the number of women who have principal licences. This number has increased from 27 per cent when they started business to 40 per cent now.

As far as opening of bank accounts is concerned, there are noticeable developments. While 37 per cent did not have any bank account for the business when they started, this proportion has decreased to only 10 per cent. At the same time, the proportion with savings and current accounts has increased from 52 per cent and 15 per cent to 65 per cent and 25 per cent respectively.

Most of the women entrepreneurs who participated in the in-depth study have formalized their business activities. Of the 9 women who started informally, 7 have acquired formal business premises; six of the 7 have obtained principal licences as well. According to the women, two reasons accounted for their decisions to formalize. First, the businesses had grown to a level where it was difficult to sustain them without being constantly harassed by tax officials. Secondly, they needed to establish formal premises and procedures in order to attract more customers. Ukweli says that it is difficult for her to sell her products to supermarkets because they demand receipts, which she cannot issue without a licence. Meritta notes that had she not relocated to formal business premises she would not have been so popular with dressing brides and bridesmaids.

As to what motivated formalization, the main reason cited by the women is profitability of the business, which gave them the confidence to commit themselves to paying rents and taxes.

3.7.2 Business Growth

Business growth is assessed in terms of changes in employment size, quality of employment, market coverage, equipment used and premises used.

(a)   Employment Size

The results revealed that the average number of workers has grown from three employees when the business started to five in the food processing and beauty and health, and six in the textile sector. This means the women's enterprises have contributed to increased jobs. Most of the employees were on permanent terms, while many of the women entrepreneurs used their close relatives as part-time workers in their own businesses. Some also used their businesses as learning grounds for their relatives.

(b)   Quality of Employment

Generally, the quality of employment in MSEs is known to be poor. Written contracts, pensions, insurance and other important employee benefits are rarely found in MSEs. The story is not very different in the women's enterprises surveyed. Whilst still only a minority (see Table 3.7), it is encouraging to see positive developments in this respect, i.e., more women are providing more benefits than when they started and they plan to develop these further in the future.

Table 3.7   Changes in Quality of Employment

When Started	Micro		Small		Total	
	Number	%	Number	%	Number	%
Maternity leave	15	11.7	16	12.5	31	24.2
Annual leave	11	8.6	14	10.9	25	19.5
Written employment contracts	2	1.6	4	3.4	6	4.8
Pension	-	-	2	1.6	2	1.6
Currently						
Maternity leave	16	12.5	18	14.1	34	26.6
Annual leave	11	8.6	17	13.3	28	21.9
Written employment contracts	3	2.4	9	7.1	12	9.5
Pension	-	-	4	3.2	4	3.2
In the Future						
Maternity leave	27	21.3	27	21.3	54	42.5
Annual leave	26	20.5	28	22.0	54	42.5
Written employment contracts	22	17.6	22	17.6	44	35.2
Pension	13	10.3	16	12.7	29	13

The in-depth interviews revealed that with time, some of the women have introduced a number of benefits primarily to motivate staff and ensure they retain them. The benefits vary from woman to woman and from business to business, but they include free lunch, free accommodation and assistance in meeting part of medical expenses. Women who have become successful see these benefits as being instrumental for retaining competent staff and hence being able to deliver quality services consistently. They also contribute to the productivity of the businesses.

Knowing the advantages resulting from improved quality of employment, many women intend to introduce maternity leave, annual leave and written contracts for their employees. Pension benefits appear to present the greatest challenge. Interestingly, there are no differences in the quality of employment between the micro and small enterprises. This may be explained by the fact that the difference in size among the enterprises categorized as "micro" and "small" is not that large.

(c)   Market coverage

Increased access to markets is also considered an aspect of upward mobility. The literature shows that most MSEs sell to their immediate locality. The results of this study show that the proportion of enterprises selling to markets outside their districts increased from 29 per cent when the business started to 79 per cent currently (Table 3.8).

Table 3.8   Geographical Expansion of Market Coverage

Geographical Expansion	When the business started		Currently	
	Frequency	%	Frequency	%
Within the district	123	98.4	122	98.4
Within the region	36	28.6	100	79.4
International Market	1	0.8	4	3.2

Note: multiple responses

(d)   Other Developments in the Enterprises

Analysis of the experiences of the 15 women who participated in the in-depth study reveals important differences in the development of their enterprises in terms of changes in scale of equipment used, type of premises used and other businesses established as a result of the woman's involvement in business. Four of the women entrepreneurs did not significantly change their businesses in these aspects. For the most part, they are still operating from home or small rented rooms. Seven of the women experienced moderate improvements in their employment level, scale of equipment and premises. The remaining four women entrepreneurs experienced significant improvements in these aspects. Urbania and Upendo, who have experienced the highest growth, started operating from home with one tailoring machine each. Now they are employing 21 and 18 people respectively and operating from formal business premises. Urbania has even formed a limited liability company for the business.

3.8   Growth Aspirations

3.8.1   Future plans

The respondents were asked to indicate their future business plans. As table 3.9 shows, a large majority of the women intend to make new investments, recruit more workers and expand the range of products within the next two years. Only a very small number (4 per cent) plan to reduce the number of workers. This shows that women entrepreneurs have growth aspirations, contrary to what is presented in some of the literature. There were no significant differences in terms of future plans between sectors.

Table 3.9   Future Business Plans

Future plan* (multiple responses)	Food processing		Health and Beauty		Textile		Total	
	Number	%	Number	%	Number	%	Number	%
Expand range of products	26	20.3	23	18.0	37	28.9	87	70.2
Make new investment	30	23.6	22	17.3	35	27.6	87	68.5
Increase number of workers	23	18	20	15.6	29	22.7	72	56.3
Decrease number of workers	3	2.4	2	1.6	-	-	5	3.9
Reduce range of products	-	-	2	1.6	1	0.8	3	2.3
No changes planned	4	3.1	2	1.6	6	4.7	12	9.4

3.8.2   Growth Aspirations in Terms of Workforce Size

In order to gauge the respondent's growth aspirations, they were asked to indicate how big they would like their businesses to be in five years' time in terms of employment size. Table 3.10 shows that about a fifth (19.1 per cent) of the women aspire to have 20 or more employees in the next five years. The largest group of respondents (45 per cent) aspires to have less than 10 employees, meaning that they would like to be running microenterprises.   There is an apparent positive relationship between current size and aspired size. The explanation for this might be that aspirations increase with size. As a business grows, the need for and viability of growth may also increase.   This means aspirations are not static. The results suggest that the women entrepreneurs have a very positive outlook on the future and plan to further develop their enterprises.

Table 3.10   Growth Aspirations in Terms of Employment Size

Current level of Employee	1 to 9		10 to 19		20 to 50 or more		Total	
	Number	%	Number	%	Number	%	Number	%
1 to 4	46	40	11	9.6	3	2.6	60	52.2
5 to 10	5	4.3	28	24.3	8	7	41	35.7
11 to 15	1	0.9	2	1.7	8	7	11	9.6
Over 15		0		0	3	2.6	3	2.6
Total	**52**	**45.2**	**41**	**35.7**	**22**	**19.1**	**115**	**100**

Consistent with the survey, the in-depth interviews revealed that the women's future aspirations vary from very modest to very substantial ones. Also, the greater the growth already achieved, the higher the aspirations. Urbania, who has developed the business from an informal part-time tailor to a limited liability company employing 21 persons, plans to start a store selling imported, quality ready-made garments. She has already carried out an assessment of the sources of supply and import procedures. Urbania's intentions shed further light on the motives for diversification. She says she does not want the tailoring business to grow beyond its current size because she does not want to deal with more employees. She says that the tailors she has "are already a headache!". Instead of increasing the size of the tailoring business, she would rather specialize in sizes and designs.

Matrona, who has developed a very successful salon and boutique, plans to start a beauty training school or college. Modesta, whose tailoring business has grown from employing one employee to five, says that the business is still in its infancy and she wants it to develop to at least double its current size. Ulkaria, who has developed the business from a lone informal hairdresser to a formally established one employing 12 persons, plans to buy the building she is operating in, add on one storey and open up a boutique. By contrast, Nana, Nestoria and Naomi, who employ a maximum of two people each, are more focused on attracting profitability and formalising their businesses. Martina is in the process of incorporating a company, under which all her businesses will operate. This should enable her to attract big tenders from government and other large institutions. She plans to start operating internationally in the future. In readiness for this, she is attending English classes to improve her mastery of the language.

3.9   Factors Favourable to Growth

Respondents were also asked to indicate factors which have facilitated growth of their enterprises. Their responses as summarized in Table 3.11 show that the most commonly cited facilitating factors are access to finance and access to equipment/working tools. Following in importance are working premises, technical skills and advertising. Sector-wise, financial ability appears to be more important in facilitating growth in the textile businesses, while technical skills are seen as least important in the health and beauty care sector. Access to equipment, on the other hand, is more important in the health and beauty care businesses.

Table 3.11: Factors Helpful for Growth

	Sector							
	Food Processing		Health and Beauty		Textile		Total	
	Number	%	Number	%	No.	%	No.	%
Financial ability	15	11.7	9	7	24	19	48	37.5
Access to equipment/working tools	6	4.7	13	10.2	8	6.3	27	21.1
Increasing premises/working space	5	3.9	4	3.1	5	3.9	14	10.9
Technical Skills	6	4.7	1	0.8	6	4.7	13	10.2
Advertising	3	2.3	3	2.3	5	3.9	11	8.6
Availability of raw material	-	-	-	-	4	3.1	4	3.1
Licensing/registration of the business	2	1.6	-	-	-	-	2	1.6
Others	2	1.6	3	2.3	4	3.1	9	7
Total	**39**	**30.5**	**33**	**25.8**	**56**	**44**	**128**	**100**

3.10   Constraints to Growth

In addition to factors facilitating growth, the respondents were asked to indicate, without prompting, the critical barriers to the development of their enterprises. They mentioned the factors as shown in Table 3.12 below.

Table 3.12   Constraints to Growth

| Barriers to growth | Sector | | | | | | Total | |
| | Food Processing | | Health and Beauty | | Textile | | | |
	Number	%	Number	%	Number	%	Number	%
Finance	10	7.8	8	6.8	11	8.6	29	22.7
Competition	5	3.9	4	3.1	7	5.5	16	12.5
Corruption	3	2.3	3	2.3	6	4.7	12	9.4
Getting good premises	4	3.1	3	2.3	5	3.9	12	9.4
Access to equipment/working tools	3	2.3	4	3.1	3	2.3	10	7.8
Harassment	2	1.6	4	3.1	4	3.1	10	7.8
Stringent licensing regulations	6	4.7	2	1.6	-	-	8	6.3
Taxes	1	0.8	1	0.8	5	3.9	7	5.5
Untrustworthy employees	1	0.8	-	-	4	3.1	5	3.9
Access to skilled workers	-	-	2	1.6	1	0.8	3	2.3
Financial demands from family	1	0.8	-	-	2	1.6	3	2.3
Access to raw materials	-	-	1	0.8	1	0.8	2	1.6
Others	3	2.3	1	0.8	7	5.5	11	8.6
Total	**39**	**30.5**	**33**	**25.8**	**56**	**43.8**	**128**	**100.0**

The results are a mirror image of the factors facilitating growth. The most critical single barrier to growth is seen as access to finance. This is followed by access to good premises and working tools. However, there are some important differences with regards to the barriers, as taxes and licensing regulations are not mentioned as major problems. In the in-depth study, these issues come out as critical barriers to all those in food processing. This again shows that barriers to development of women entrepreneurs affect sectors differently.

Many of the women said that one problem which affects their business is the need for them and their employees to attend to social and traditional / cultural commitments such as wedding ceremonies, funerals and attending to the sick. The high incidence of HIV/AIDS was also noted as contributing to absenteeism among employees who have to take care of their sick relatives.

The respondents were also asked what problems, if any, smaller firms face which are not shared by larger ones? The most commonly cited problem was that small enterprises are overtaxed (Table 3.13). This is not surprising because micro and small enterprises, most of which have no audited accounts, pay fixed income tax regardless of whether they make or lose money. Also, there is no adequate differentiation in terms of licence fee depending on the level of business or location. A substantial tailoring business located in the city centre pays the same licence fee as one located in a poor suburb. Other problems cited included frequent harassment by law enforcement agencies and competition.

Table 3.13 Special Problems of Small Firms Compared to Larger Ones

Special Small Business problems	Food Processing		Health and Beauty		Textile		Total	
	Number	%	Number	%	Number	%	Number	%
Overtax	6	4.7	4	3.1	16	12.5	26	20.3
Licensing fees	4	3.1	5	3.9	4	3.1	13	10.2
Harassment	5	3.9	-	-	5	3.9	10	7.8
Production not valued	1	0.8	4	3.1	3	2.3	8	6.3
Access to finance	1	0.8	3	2.3	4	3.1	8	6.3
Regulations	4	3.1	1	0.8	1	0.8	6	4.7
Marketing problems	3	2.3	-	-	2	1.6	5	3.9
Access to premises	1	.8	-	-	2	1.6	3	2.3
Others	9	7.0	2	1.6	4	3.1	15	11.7
Non-Response	5	3.9	14	10.9	15	11.7	34	26.6
Total	**39**	**30.5**	**33**	**25.8**	**56**	**43.8**	**128**	**100.0**

Laws and regulations governing some sectors are also difficult to comply with. Most of the women engaged in food processing are unable to meet licensing requirements. Close to 2000 people have been trained by the UNIDO-supported project, but very few have been able to run formal businesses due to the stringent food processing regulations.

All the women involved in food processing who participated in the in-depth study indicated that the Food Control Act is extremely difficult to comply with for two reasons. First, the investment required to acquire land and a building which meets licensing requirements are out of reach of the women. Related to this is the fact that rents for the few facilities available are too high for their microenterprises. Even if one has the money to put up a building, there is no serviced land available for developers. This is because the government has not been fast enough to survey and service land for industrial purposes, and as a result there is a serious shortage. Most of the women in the food-processing sector interviewed are therefore operating informally, and their businesses are always at the mercy of the tax, health and licensing officers.

Ukweli and Meriana, who have experienced upward mobility in terms of employees, premises and facilities, are still operating informally, gradually building their capacity to formalize. Nevertheless, being informal puts them at a number of disadvantages, including not being free to advertise or not being able to sell to some customers who demand receipts. When there is an official operation for netting tax evaders, the women are forced to temporarily suspend business activities for some hours or even days. Meriana feels guilty when her customers ask her about the safety of her products, because she does not have an operating licence or the approval of the Ministry of Health.

The women generally perceive that tax and local government officials deliberately harass them in order to extort bribes from them. They do this by deliberately overstating the tax liability in order that the woman negotiates with them. Urbania reports that once they estimated her annual tax liability at US $ 20,000. When she asked for the basis for the estimate, the officer replied that she drives expensive cars and travels abroad. Later they asked her to pay them US $ 2,000 as a bribe so they could reduce the liability to US $ 1,000. Respondents reported many instances where tax officials took away their working tools because the women had not paid the taxes which the officials were demanding. This necessitated closing the business for up to a week in order to regain the equipment. On some occasions, these tools were damaged while in the hands of the officials and there is no compensation for such damage.

Two of the women entrepreneurs narrated incidences where local government officials took away dryers from their salons. For four days Urbania could not work. Nana's story is different:

> "The city officials came to my business to ask for a licence which I had not renewed. I told them that I was in the process of getting it. They decided to take my dryer which was the main source of getting my clients. This forced me to close the salon for some days in order to follow up for the dryer. As I was following up I was told that I have to offer something to get back my dryer. I told the people I had just started my business so I did not get a lot of money. They told me if you don't have money you can pay in-kind. At first I did not understand what they meant but later I knew what it was. The mere fact I had closed the business for a week, I lost my customers. I decided not to offer myself, but that meant me closing my business. As you see me now I am trying it for the second time. Unfortunately without the right equipment and facilities many customers do not come to me. What I have learnt this time is that I will make sure I pay all what is required, but for the time being I will operate informally until when I can meet all the costs required".

While Urbania managed to continue with her business, Nana has not recovered from the loss. Urbania could continue with her business because when the tailoring business was closed for four days she still operated the hair business. Unfortunately Nana had only the hair salon as the sole source of income.

3.11 Incidents which have Negatively Effected Women Enterprises

Respondents were asked to mention critical incidents which had negatively affected their businesses. Table 3.14 below shows that theft had affected about a quarter of the businesses. The most affected sector was textiles. The "other" factors include such issues as harassment by health officers, drastic increases in rent forcing the woman to relocate, power disconnection after delays in paying their electricity bills, death of a key supporter, drunken men storming into a salon and causing damage to property, etc.

Table 3.14 Critical Incidents Affecting Business Negatively

Critical Incidence	Food Processing		Health and Beauty		Textile		Total	
	Number	%	Number	%	Number	%	Number	%
Theft	3	2.3	7	5.5	21	16.4	31	24.2
Sickness	2	1.6	1	0.8	3	2.3	6	4.7
Lack of skills	-	-	3	2.3	3	2.3	6	4.7
Lack of Utilities	1	0.8	4	3.1	1	0.8	6	4.7
Premises	-	-	-	-	3	2.3	3	2.3
Others	13	10.2	5	3.9	8	6.3	26	20.3
Non response	20	15.6	13	10.2	17	13.3	50	39.1
Total	**39**	**30.5**	**33**	**25.8**	**56**	**43.8**	**128**	**100.0**

3.12 Gender-Related Constraints

One interest of the study was to assess whether the difficulties or successes experienced by women entrepreneurs are gender-related. To answer this question, the women were requested to indicate whether there are situations where the business environment affects women entrepreneurs differently than their male counterparts. More than a quarter of the women entrepreneurs indicated that the problems they experience in running their businesses were related to gender.

Table 3.15 Are there Issues Affecting Women Entrepreneurs Differently?

Region	Yes		No		Total	
	Number	%	Number	%	Number	%
Dar es Salaam	20	15.6	45	35.1	65	50.8
Arusha	10	7.8	26	20.3	36	28.1
Zanzibar	4	3.1	20	15.6	24	18.8
No response	0	0	0	0	3	2.3
Total	**34**	**26.6**	**91**	**71**	**128**	**100.0**

All but one of the women who participated in the in-depth study initially indicated that there are no problems affecting them because they are women. However, upon probing, many acknowledged that there are such factors. For example, Ulkaria had initially said that there are no gender-related problems facing her. Later, however, she admitted that she spends much less time on the business that she would have, if she did not have to take care of household chores and other responsibilities.

Upendo says that she has to make sure that she prepares the children to go to school. She has to prepare breakfast for them and their father. When they have left the house, she prepares herself to go to the business. Instead of starting work at 8.00 like others, she often starts at between 9 and 11 a.m. Also, she could work up to 5.00 p.m., but because of her family responsibilities at home she has to close at 4.00 p.m. This leaves her with just 6 hours of work. By comparison, some of the other people in the tailoring business she knows work up to 10 hours. Interestingly, none of the other women indicated that she works so few hours.

During maternity leave, the businesses owned by women can suffer because they often remain without adequate management in the absence of the woman owner. As a response, women sometimes close their businesses. This also affects their clientele.

Another gender-related problem is that some of the officials and business people who deal with the women entrepreneurs do not trust that the women can meet their contractual obligations and hence try to work through the husbands. Ukweli, engaged in food processing, reports that some of the suppliers prefer to negotiate with her husband when it comes to matters related to the business. Sometimes she starts discussions with a supplier of packaging materials, but the supplier insists that he will conclude the deal with her husband. She thinks that some suppliers doubt whether she can pay for the order and prefer to deal with her husband whom they wrongly think is the one who will pay them. This sometimes leads to a situation where the husband makes inappropriate decisions, because he is not involved in the day-to-day activities of the business and does not always have enough time to consult her.

Some women are harassed by their spouses while doing business. Martina reports that her former husband supported her at the beginning by giving her capital. He also took care of all family needs from his salary, leaving her to spend or re-invest whatever she earned. However when she started earning some good money, he changed. He would sometimes come to the business and quarrel with her, making a lot of noise. This very much affected the business, since many customers did not like the husband's behaviour. Eventually, she decided to separate from the husband. Martina has now learnt to stand on her own.

4. Use and Impact of Support Services

4.1 Access to and Use of Financial Services

Table 4.1 shows the extent to which women entrepreneurs had tried to access credit and their success in doing so. The Table shows that a large proportion (41 per cent) of the women tried to access loans from MFIs, and that many of them were successful.

Table 4.1   Attempts to Access Finance and Incidence of Success

Source	Tried to access credit		Successful	
	Number	%	Number	%
Dar es Salaam				
Micro-Finance Institution (MFIs)	28	21.9	20	15.6
Friend and Family members	26	20.3	18	14.1
Bank	12	9.4	6	4.7
Money lender	4	3.1	3	2.3
Arusha				
Micro-Finance Institution (MFIs)	19	14.8	16	12.5
Friend and Family members	10	7.8	9	7.0
Bank	16	12.5	8	6.3
Money lender	3	2.3	2	1.6
Zanzibar				
Micro-Finance Institution (MFIs)	6	4.7	4	3.1
Bank	1	0.8	1	0.8
Friend and Family members	1	0.8	1	0.8
Money lender	-	-	-	-
Total				
Micro-Finance Institution (MFIs)	53	41.4	40	31.3
Friend and Family members	37	28.9	28	21.9
Bank	29	22.7	15	11.7
Money lender	7	5.5	5	3.9

About a quarter of respondents tried to get loans from banks, half of whom were successful. A good number of the women got loans from friends and families. Notwithstanding the successes in getting loans, those who had attempted to borrow money indicated that they had faced a number of problems, and the main issues are shown in Table 4.2.

Table 4.2: Problems Faced in Borrowing Money

Constraint	Sector						Total	
	Food Processing		Health and Beauty		Textile			
	Number	%	Number	%	Number	%	Number	%
Cumbersome procedures	12	9.4	6	4.7	15	11.7	33	25.8
High interest rates	10	7.8	5	3.9	12	9.4	27	21.1
Small loan size	7	5.5	3	2.3	12	9.4	22	17.2
Lack of collateral	5	3.9	2	1.6	6	4.7	13	10.2
Inability to write business plan	2	1.6	-	-	2	1.6	4	3.1
Total	**39**	**30.5**	**33**	**25.8**	**56**	**43.8**	**128**	**100**

The most commonly cited problems are cumbersome procedures and high interest rates. These are followed by small loan sizes from MFIs and lack of collateral in the case of bank loans. The women who participated in the in-depth study gave a number of reasons why it is difficult to access finance. First, the banks require borrowers to have collateral worth at least 125 per cent of the amount borrowed. The women were unable to provide collateral and therefore only two of them (Ulkaria and Urbania) have been able to access bank loans.

Secondly, the banks are not accustomed to dealing with small businesses and as such see them as very risky. Matrona says that when she approached the bank officials for a loan, they concentrated more on the collateral she would provide than on the history and performance of the business, which she believes should be the most important factor in making a lending decision. The third problem is that banks charge about 25-30 per cent interest for loans to small enterprises and the women entrepreneurs consider this to be very expensive.

An alternative to bank loans is borrowing from Micro-Finance Institutions (MFIs). These institutions have two limitations. First, one has to start borrowing very small amounts and gradually graduate to higher sums. The amount they start lending (about US $50) is considered too low to be of much use to most of the women interested in growing their own businesses. Secondly, MFIs require the borrowers to attend weekly meetings which takes a lot of their working time.

Nana, the least upwardly mobile of the women, says that the MFIs are of no help. She sites FINCA, which operates in Mkanyageni where she runs her business. She finds the initial loan amount provided (US $60) too small to help her business to grow. Also, she could not raise the weekly repayment of US$ 5.20 from her business. She also argues that the loan is not even enough to pay for licence. To get the licence she has to pay US $50 as a licence fee, US $10 for the health permit, and US $3.40 as an application fee. Therefore the total amount required to formalize the business is US $ 63.50, which is more than the loan US $60 offered by the MFI.

Nana is also aware of PRIDE (T) which offers loans with smaller repayment instalments than those offered by FINCA, but she says to get the loan one has to take a bus to

Magomeni for which she has to pay US $0.60 per day. Before she gets a loan she has to attend eight meetings, which will cost US $4.80 in bus fares. She thinks her problems are beyond her ability to solve, and it will be difficult to take a loan from such financial institutions.

Although both men and women face the problem of access to finance, it is affects women more for a number of reasons. First, women have less access to property, which can be pledged as collateral. This is due to property laws and traditional customs which deny women control over property. Meritta was refused a loan because she did not have any property of her own to pledge. Meriana, a woman engaged in food processing and struggling to formalize, has build her own house, using her own income. When she wanted to pledge it as collateral she consulted the family (including her in-laws) first. They categorically refused to allow her to pledge it, saying that the house is a very important asset for the family and should not be pledged as collateral. This means that even if the laws allow women to have the same rights over property as men, unless customs and traditions change, some women will continue having no real control over property.

Secondly, bank officials are said to treat women-owned businesses differently. Matrona thinks that the bank officers do not consider women seriously. She says when men go to a bank they are taken seriously, but when women apply for loans they are not treated seriously. Bank officials doubt whether a woman can repay the loan. They fear that a woman will not use the money for her business. However, Urbania, the most upwardly mobile of the women, thinks that banks do not discriminate against women. She feels that some women are not serious about their businesses and so the banks ignore them.

4.2   Access to and Use of Business Support Services

Table 4.3 summarizes the services accessed by women entrepreneurs. Training in business management is the most commonly received service, followed by technical training in food processing and training in marketing. All of those who have reported receiving these services also indicated that the services have had a positive impact on their businesses.

Table 4.3   Services Accessed by the Women Entrepreneurs

Services accessed	Food Processing		Health and Beauty		Textile		Total	
	Number	%	Number	%	Number	%	Number	%
Training in business management	10	7.8	15	11.7	17	13.3	42	32.8
Technical training [Food processing]	16	12.5	-	-	6	4.7	22	17.2
Training in marketing	4	3.1	2	1.6	10	7.8	16	12.5
Other technical training	2	1.6	-	-	7	5.5	9	7.0
Training in Record / Book-Keeping	-	-	2	1.6	4	3.1	6	4.7
Other services	7	5.5	14	10.9	12	9.4	33	25.8
Total	**39**	**30.5**	**33**	**25.8**	**56**	**43.8**	**128**	**100.0**

The access to and impact of training in business skills, technical skills and marketing (trade fairs, advertising, etc.) was analyzed further through the in-depth interviews.

4.2.1 Business Skills Development

Of the 15 women entrepreneurs interviewed in the in-depth study, all of those in food processing had attended a business skills training course organized by the UNIDO-supported food processing programme and / or TAFOPA, their association. For the women in textile and beauty services, only Upendo has attended such training, a two-week course organized by Poverty Africa. However, she could not afford the time to complete the training, due to commitments at home and the fact that some of her most important clients wanted their clothes to be produced by her personally. Meritta and Matrona have heard of the availability of training, but they say they cannot afford the time required to attend because some customers insist on being served by them personally, and they cannot afford to lose them.

Some women entrepreneurs have overcome this problem by hiring expert tailors from the Democratic Republic of Congo (DRC), who are accepted by most clients. However, this is only possible for women who have already established themselves sufficiently to pay the high salaries which employees from DRC or other places demand. Tailors and beauty clinicians who are growing their businesses, will continue to face serious difficulties in relation to being able to leave their businesses and attend training.

Part of the problem is that the training offered to MSE operators is perceived as too basic for the relatively advanced women entrepreneurs. For example, Matrona, has studied commercial subjects at secondary school and has been training other women in tailoring at the Vocational Education and Training Authority (VETA) centre. Once she tried to lease tailoring machines, but the NGO which was leasing them, required her to attend a related course for two weeks. When she looked at the contents of the course, she found them to be too basic to be of any use to her. She thought she already knew much more than what they had to offer, and could not afford to be away from her business for two weeks <u>and</u> not learn anything new. She decided not to attend the course and hence was not able to lease the equipment. Matrona laments that many organizations which are supporting women entrepreneurs, think that all women are looking for the basics, when in fact some women have achieved a degree of development and are only constrained from developing further because of lack of appropriate and often "advanced" support.

4.2.2 Technical Skills Development

All the women engaged in food processing covered by the in-depth study had received support in terms of technical skills from the UNIDO-supported food-processing programme. The programme has also been designing, ordering and selling packaging materials and labels to women who attended the training. The women use the common labels until they are able to meet the costs of ordering labels for their own businesses. In addition, they get on-site visits and advice from the trainers of the programme. Women in food processing who benefited from this project report that it was instrumental in helping them to establish and develop their businesses. Of the four women who have gone through the programme, three have already designed and started using their own labels. In order to maintain some legitimacy, they print the TAFOPA logo on all their labels.

So far there is no institution in Tanzania involved in the technical skills development for women in beauty care although this is one of the sectors where many women are engaged in, especially in urban areas. They rely on foreign expertise and technical training by the cosmetics suppliers on how to use their products.

Some of the women engaged in the beauty care sector obtained their training by going to neighboring countries including Kenya. The Vocational Education and Training Authority (VETA) which is the training and apprenticeship training institution for Tanzania does not provide training in this sector.

4.2.3 Trade Fairs

The women entrepreneurs in food processing, as well as some of those in tailoring, have also benefited from various trade fairs organized by Tanzania Gatsby Trust (TGT), the Small Industry Development Organization (SIDO), Equal Opportunity for all Trust Fund (EOTF), and other local and international organizations. The information on these fairs is often communicated to them through the UNIDO-supported food processing programme, or through their sectoral associations.

The women who had attended trade fairs reported that these events had been very useful in exposing them to ideas, as well as in creating awareness and increasing sales of their products. Ukweli and Meriana reported that they met most of their big customers during trade fairs. However, they lamented that the fairs are always very long in duration (7-10 days) and they cost a lot in terms of subsistence. It is also difficult for them, as women, to go to trade fairs for that long, leaving behind their children, spouses and other family members. As a result, they have started using assistants to attend the trade fairs.

4.2.4 Marketing Services, Information and Advice

Some of the women seem to be missing business opportunities due to not having information or not being aware of them. There are also few mechanisms in place for providing basic marketing information or advice to women entrepreneurs. For example, Upendo makes attractive and innovative dolls in Arusha town. For months, she used to sell these to boys passing by her tailoring shop at very low prices. She later found her dolls being sold to tourists at 10 times what she was charging. She has now set up her own stall to sell the dolls at the tourist market. When asked whether she had explored the possibility of selling her products to supermarkets or other shops in large quantities, she said that she was not aware that they would buy toys from her, but would be glad if someone could connect her to such buyers.

4.2.5 Advertising

Some of the women have made use of advertising services, though these were not targeted specifically at assisting MSEs. For example, Meritta, a tailor located in Arusha, advertises her business in "Mererani", a local weekly newspaper in Arusha municipality. She also uses postcards to send greetings through the radio and announces that the greetings come from her salon. In this way she has generated awareness and interest in her business among many clients.

4.3   The Role of Business Associations

Generally, there are few business associations focused on women. These include Tanzania Food Processors' Association (TAFOPA) and Federation of Association of Women Entrepreneurs in Tanzanian (FAWETA). As shown in Tables 4.4 and 4.5, many women are not aware of the business associations and few are members of such associations. Some consider these associations as having been started by individuals with the purpose of personal gain, and not for the interest of women entrepreneurs more generally.

Table 4.4   Women Entrepreneurs' Awareness of Associations

| Type/Name of Association | Sectors | | | | | | Total | |
| | Food Processing | | Textile | | Beauty | | | |
	Number	%	Number	%	Number	%	Number	%
TCCIA	26	20.3	35	27.3	15	11.7	76	59.4
TAFOPA	31	24.2	20	15.6	10	61	61	47.7
FAWETA	22	17.2	19	14.8	6	4.7	47	36.7
VIBINDO	17	13.3	22	17.2	6	4.7	45	35.2
National Business Council	11	8.6	6	4.7	4	21	21	16.4
Private Sector Foundation	8	6.3	9	7.0	3	20	20	15.6

The women's incidence of membership to various associations is summarized in Table 4.5 below.

Table 4.5   Women Entrepreneurs' Membership of Associations

| Type/Name of Associations | Sectors | | | | | | | |
| | Food Processing | | Textile | | Beauty | | Total | |
	Number	%	Number	%	Number	%	Number	%
TAFOPA	25	19.5	1	0.8	1	0.8	27	21.8
TCCIA	4	3.1	3	2.3	-	-	7	5.5
FAWETA	3	2.3	2	1.6	-	-	5	3.9
VIBINDO	1	0.8	-	-	1	0.8	2	1.6
Total	33	25.7	6	4.7	2	1.6	41	32.8

Asked why they were not members of the business associations, the women entrepreneurs gave the reasons presented in Table 4.6. The main factor contributing to the lack of participation is the women's lack of awareness about these associations.

Table 4.6   Reasons for not Being Members of Associations

Reasons	Number	%
I am not aware of the associations	78	81.3
Others	9	9.4
They do not provide any meaningful benefits/waste of time	4	4.2
I need to know them better first	3	3.1
High membership fees	2	2.1
Total	**75**	**100.0**

However, with the 15 women interviewed, further probing revealed that many women entrepreneurs who were not members of associations thought that the associations were there for larger, more established enterprises.

TAFOPA members have significantly benefited from their association. They operate semi-formally (strictly speaking illegally) relatively freely because of their membership to the association. The association has been negotiating with some government officials to allow small-scale (informal) food processors to continue operating so as to build their own capacity to meet the food processing standards.

Modesta, who is a member of TCCIA, encourages women to join associations because she has been getting information on local and international trade fairs, training and study tour opportunities from TCCIA and these have been very beneficial to her business. She says that she got most of her customers for her artefacts from trade fairs, and information about the fairs is communicated to her by TCCIA.

Upendo is not a member of any association. Neither has she heard of any. She however doubts whether she would be able to spare time to attend to matters of such organizations, given that she is already very busy with her business. Nana, one of the least upwardly mobile of the women, does not know any women's business organizations, but she thinks these organizations could be of help to women entrepreneurs if they knew about them.

Other women entrepreneurs who have not joined associations have very negative perceptions of these organizations. For example, Matilda thinks that the associations operate on the basis of favouritism and nepotism. She cites a bad experience with SUWATA, a defunct women's organization. The leadership had offered the women a chance to display their products on a weekly basis on the understanding that they would later be facilitated to travel overseas to participate in a trade fair. The organization did not keep its promise. She believes many organizations purporting to help women entrepreneurs are out to exploit them. Margareth, who does not belong to any association, concurs arguing that founders and leaders of many associations are cliques of well-connected individuals who have their own agenda, and they just use other women as a cover.

The experience of Narcia, one of the food processors, supports the notion that members of associations do not benefit equally from them. Narcia was the founder member and regional chairperson of a women's organization. After passing on leadership to younger women, they started sidelining her and as a result she no longer gets information about meetings or any support from the association, and this has affected her business negatively. She believes that she has been marginalized, not because she is a woman, but because she is poor. She believes that the wives of the powerful people, who are now leading the association, face different types of problems from poor women like her and therefore don't see why they should work with her. She strongly believes that poor women cannot benefit from an association which is dominated by leaders who are wives of well-to-do persons, since they do not share the same types of problems. She advises that there should be different associations for different categories of women.

4.4   Family and the Business

The families of the women entrepreneurs have played a key role in the development of the enterprises. In many cases, spouses have been supportive and their financial and moral support have been instrumental in the establishment and development of the business. In some cases, spouses have been discouraging women from developing their businesses. Meriana's husband discouraged her from starting a business, telling her that she could not run one successfully. However, now that she has demonstrated that she can, he is very supportive of her. If this is a common occurance, there could be many women in Tanzania who have the potential to develop successful enterprises, but who have been discouraged from doing so by their spouses, who wrongly think that the women cannot make it.

Some men do not have confidence in their wives' ability to run formal business activities and therefore discourage them from formalising. For example, both Urbania and Meritta started running their businesses informally from home. When they wanted to rent formal premises and acquire licences, their husbands were against their plans, arguing that the women would not be able to sustain the licence fees and taxes involved. The women decided to go ahead and now they are successful and much appreciated and supported by their husbands. Had the women not decided to go against their spouses' preferences, they would very likely still be operating micro-enterprise activities informally. This suggests there may be many women entrepreneurs whose businesses remain informal because the husbands discourage them from formalising them.

Matilda, a bag maker, says that she consults her spouse about many of the things she does. She says that:

> "I know I am doing well because I rely on God, but also thanks to my supportive and understanding husband. She advises married women who do business to be open to their husbands She says, "If you are married and you are doing business and you want to become successful then do not hide anything from your husband and don't claim whatever you have is yours alone. Everything should be shared"

5. Strategies Adopted by Successful Women Entrepreneurs

Women entrepreneurs who manage to develop small informal enterprises adopt a number of strategies to deal with the challenges facing them. These strategies are discussed in the following sections.

5.1 Accessing Finance

5.1.1 Alternative Forms of Collateral
The women who have successfully accessed bank loans used a number of alternative forms of collateral. Urbania wanted to borrow money from the bank, but she did not have an asset which she could pledge as collateral. She convinced a relative to allow her to use his house as collateral. After that she worked very hard and saved up US $ 20,000 in a fixed deposit. She then used it as collateral. With the account as collateral, she is charged an interest of 6 per cent instead of the normal 25 per cent.

5.1.2 Planning Ahead

Ulkaria is planning to gradually buy the house she is currently renting, so that she can use it as security for borrowing money to meet future investment needs.

5.1.3 Creative use of MFIs
Despite the criticisms of MFIs noted earlier, a number of the women creatively made use of this source of finance. After realising that she could not afford to attend the borrowers' meetings, Ulkaria, who runs a beauty salon in Arusha appointed one of her trustworthy employees to attend the weekly meetings. She also did not use the money she borrowed in the first rounds because it was of no use to her, given her business needs. Instead, she used the money to quickly repay her loans and hence move up the ladder in terms of amounts she could borrow. She used this trick until she was eligible to borrow 1 million shillings, which she used to buy dryers for her salon. Later, she used the dryers as collateral to support her application for a loan to the National Micro-Finance Bank.

Martina says that one way of minimising the need for borrowing is to carefully manage cash. She says she does this by avoiding keeping cash at home. She quickly banks or promptly reinvests all monies received in the business, in order to avoid the temptation to spend them on other things.

5.2 Dealing with Unfriendly Laws and Regulations

The women who have successfully developed their businesses have used a number of strategies to deal with unfriendly laws and regulations. Margareth, Matrona and Martina say that they are very firm when dealing with tax officials, sending a clear message that they are not ready to pay any bribes. They say that when the officials know you are strong, they stop harassing you. Urbania says that she keeps her records and gets her accounts audited, and this makes it difficult for the tax people to harass her. Some of the women admitted that sometimes they are forced to bribe the tax officials in order not to waste too much time or lose business, through, for example their equipment being confiscated.

The women engaged in food processing use labels which show that they are members of TAFOPA. This helps to give the products some form of legitimacy in the eyes of consumers.

5.3 Competition in the Market

Those women entrepreneurs who have growing businesses had adopted a number of deliberate marketing strategies. They include cultivating knowledge about the needs and tastes of their customers; focusing on the quality of their services and maintaining quality; advertising their services in mass media; attending trade fairs; recruiting and retaining highly qualified staff (sometimes from outside the country), and motivating their employees to deliver the best service possible. Meritta and Alex have been advertising their salons on the radio and in newspapers in Arusha municipality. Since radio adverts are expensive, Meritta has resorted to buying greeting cards and sending greetings from her salon. This has increased awareness and interest in her salon. Martina, Urbania, Ulkaria and Matrona have all employed experts from Democratic Republic of Congo. They are highly paid, but these women believe that it is worth it. Ulkaria, Margareth, Meritta and Urbania have been attending beauty-related courses in Kenya, as well as those organized locally by the cosmetics suppliers on usage of their products.

5.4 Competing for Skilled Employees

The women have also developed a number of strategies to attract and retain skilled workers. First, they have introduced incentives in the form of good salaries and other benefits to staff. Almost all of the women who have developed their businesses provide free lunch to their staff. Some also provide annual leave. Urbania provides a 30-day paid leave to all staff from 20th December to 20th January every year. She notes that employees report back to work in January refreshed. Martina provides accommodation to all staff who do not mind staying in a room provided by her. Having found it difficult to retain some specialized tailors, Martina has resorted to sub-contracts for some work and has one tailor whom she pays on a piecework basis.

5.5 Managing Multiple Roles

To deal with multiple roles and demands on their time from family members, the women have adopted a number of strategies. Ukweli, Naomi, Meritta, Upendo and Ulkaria have deliberately decided to focus their efforts on a few activities, in order to be effective and at the same time attend to their responsibilities at home. Modesta has been taking the children to the business to see what she is doing and how busy she is, so that they reduce demands on her to be at home for longer periods.

5.6 Obtaining Support and Co-operation of Family

Married women deliberately cultivate the trust, confidence and co-operation of their spouses by making sure that they are open and transparent to their husbands regarding all their activities and their movements. This helps minimize any elements of suspicion, which might prompt the spouse to restrict the woman's movements or working hours.

6. Conclusions and Proposed Interventions

6.1 Conclusions

6.1.1 Profile and motivation for starting businesses

The common view of women entrepreneurs in the MSE sector in Tanzania is that they have limited education, limited experience as well as very limited access to resources, and that they start business principally out of economic necessity. The findings of this study show that this is not the case for many women entrepreneurs. A number of the women have secondary or higher education and work experience, and are able to access finance and advice from their relatives, including their spouses. Also while some start business out of economic necessity, a large number are also motivated by other factors including financial security in the event that the spouse is unable to provide for the family; having control over resources; having an interest in the kind of activity the business is doing; gaining the respect and status in the family which comes with success in running a business, etc.

6.1.2 Extent to which Women Entrepreneurs Aspire to and Grow their Businesses

The study found that some women entrepreneurs aspire to and actually achieve significant growth of their businesses. The research has shown that there are women who manage to start informal, microenterprises, many of which are started on a part-time basis or as hobbies, and they develop them into serious formal entities, employing significant numbers of people (an average of 9 per women entrepreneur). In addition to the direct employment which they provide to employees, the women engage the labour of family members and provide significant apprenticeship opportunities. Most of the businesses are also incrementally developing in terms of the scale and sophistication of their equipment and premises. There is no doubt that women can develop successful enterprises that provide employment for others.

The results also show that many women pro-actively plan for the future development of their businesses. This is clearly demonstrated by their plans to introduce new products, enter new markets, increase production volume, acquire more equipment and bigger premises, or even start other larger businesses. It is also clear that women entrepreneurs' aspirations are not static: they change (often increase) with the development of the business. It is also found that upward mobility can take place by either developing the existing business activity, or by starting other bigger or more profitable business activities.

The study has also shown that women entrepreneurs develop their businesses in a considered way. Decisions to increase or limit the size of activities or diversify to other types of activities are reached after taking into account the resources they have; their needs; alternatives available in case a business fails; responsibilities which they have; their interests; their experiences, etc.

6.1.3 Constraints to growth

The constraints to growth found by this study are similar to those reported in the previous studies, such as limited access to finance, premises and skills; cultural values which are not conducive to successful operation of MSEs, unfriendly laws and regulations which are difficult to comply with, and corruption. There are however differences in the way these affect women entrepreneurs, and in particular this segment of women entrepreneurs who are growing businesses.

- **Access to finance**. For growing MSEs, the problem of access to finance is not availability per se, but being able to access loan sizes appropriate to the needs of their enterprises. This is because the women in growing MSEs need relatively large loans, which are not available from MFIs. Most of the women entrepreneurs are unable to borrow from banks because they demand collateral, which the women do not have. There is a need to introduce a broader range of financial products which are accessible to women growing their own MSEs.

- **Shortage of skilled labour.** There are some skills for which there is a very limited local supply. These include specialized skills in tailoring (e.g. fashion design) and beauty care. As a result, even MSEs are importing labour to fill this gap. There is therefore a need to develop local capacity for the skills required in MSEs, so as to avail of more employment opportunities for the local population.

- **Access to training**. Some women are unable to attend training organized in conventional workshops, mainly because the activities they are engaged in require them to work on the business continuously. This suggests the need for training approaches which can effectively reach the women at their work places, such as through radio programmes.

- **Laws and regulations.** Some women entrepreneurs are unable to formalize their businesses because of stringent requirements in terms of premises which can be licenced for production activities. This is especially the case among those in food processing, most of whom remain informal because they cannot afford the high cost of building or renting premises which are appropriate for the size of their business. There is a need to provide facilities for women entrepreneurs in this sector to be able to develop their activities up to a point where they can rent or establish their own facilities.

6.1.4 Gender-related constraints

There are a number of specific gender-related constraints which negatively affect women entrepreneurs' success. Difficulties in accessing bank finance due to lack of property rights and hence collateral; underestimation of women's capacity to borrow and repay by bank officials; time pressures due to multiple caring roles at home, in the community and in the business, and women being subjected to pressure to give sexual favours to corrupt officials are commonly cited issues by the women. The study has however shed some new light on some of these issues. For example, it is apparent that even where women legally own property, cultural values may not allow them to pledge this as collateral, as they still have to secure the permission of their family members.

It is also clear from the findings that, while men can be very supportive to women entrepreneurs, husbands can also present a serious hindrance to their spouses' development by underestimating their capabilities and hence discouraging them from taking risks and developing substantial enterprises. Indeed, the results of this study show that in some cases, women are much more willing to take risks than their husbands are prepared to allow them. If such attitudes prevail, there could be many women in Tanzania who are operating far below their potential. This suggests that men need to be sensitized to allow and actually encourage their spouses to start and develop businesses, rather than doing the opposite.

Another interesting phenomenon is the situation where some of those who contract with the businesses want to deal with a man, usually the husband, even when the husband does not know what is going on in that business. This can lead to counter-productive decisions by the husband. Women and men need to know how to deal with situations like this, without upsetting their clients or suppliers.

Perhaps the most serious family-related problem is the direct harassment by spouses who feel insecure due to the success of their wives. Such a situation is sure to ruin the business if it is not properly managed.

The results have shown that some of the problems that women face arise from their actual and perceived economic position in society. Also, while associations can be very helpful, they can also become a vehicle by which economically strong women can team up to capitalize on opportunities provided by the association, to the detriment of some poorer members. It is important to remember that while women entrepreneurs are generally marginalized, other women can further marginalize them. MSE development programmes and business associations should take this into consideration.

6.1.5 Strategies Adopted by Successful Women Entrepreneurs

Women who have managed to develop their enterprises have done so by using a number of innovative strategies. For every challenge that the women entrepreneurs face, some have managed to successfully address it in one way or another. This has two implications. First, it is clear that women differ in their capacities to deal with challenges that they face, and those who manage to come up with effective strategies succeed. Secondly, the strategies that they have adopted are appropriate to the situation facing them. However, this study was limited to three sectors. It is quite possible that a more detailed analysis of strategies used in other sectors could unearth a wealth of other lessons, which can gainfully be adopted by other women entrepreneurs.

6.1.6 Role of the Support Environment

Access by women entrepreneurs to business support services, including technical and business training, finance and associations varies widely. Such support appears to have significant positive impact on the women's businesses. However, not all sectors have the same access to support, and access appears limited for beauty-care services. Also, there is little support for specialized services in tailoring (fashion design for example). As a result, experts in these fields have to be imported from other countries, which is expensive, as well as taking up jobs that could otherwise be taken up by locals.

Generally, support available to MSEs is designed for the needs of microenterprises and consequently those businesses that are growing have difficulties making use of this support. It should be noted that both new and growing MSEs contribute to employment creation. Therefore there is a need to design support programmes specifically appropriate to the needs of "growing MSEs", as well as for those in the start-up stage. For example, while women face serious difficulties in marketing and accessing market information, there are few institutions which provide such specialist services.

It is clear from the findings that family support contributes significantly to the development of MSEs. However, this is not taken into consideration in the design of many MSE support programmes. Tapping family support can be a very cost-effective way of contributing to the development of women-owned enterprises.

Early socialization of children seems to have a significant affect on their choice of future careers. It is important therefore to encourage women entrepreneurs to deliberately socialize their children to the activities they are engaged in, so that the children can develop the skills, interest and motivation to be successful entrepreneurs.

6.2   Proposed Interventions

Based on the findings reported and conclusions made above, a number of interventions were proposed by the team of national consultants, UDEC, to speed up the process of development and growth for women-owned enterprises from informal micro-level activities to formal, small-scale and medium-scale enterprises in Tanzania.

6.2.1 Capacity Building of Women's Business Associations

Although associations provide many opportunities for women to develop their activities, existing women entrepreneurs' organizations are weak, most are unknown to the women interviewed, or are perceived by some women as being of little use. Women in some sectors, such as beauty care, are still not organized and do not have a trade association. It is recommended to set up a support programme for promoting the networking of women entrepreneurs with the option of developing such associations. The programme should support the formation and strengthening of women's associations especially in the fields of marketing, organization and governance so that they can attract enough members to become effective in advocacy, provision of services to members, and eventually become financially sustainable. Lessons should be carefully drawn from previous attempts to support women organizations in Tanzania. The Ministry of Industry and Trade could design this programme in association with a local business development services (BDS) provider, with the possibility of technical and financial support from the International Labour Organization (ILO) as part of its support for women's entrepreneurship development in Tanzania.

6.2.2 Strengthening Women Entrepreneurs' Business Skills and Gender Awareness

It is clear from the findings that many women entrepreneurs cannot follow conventional training programmes because of their work schedules at home and at their businesses. It is therefore recommended to design and offer training courses on how to manage businesses, and such courses should have a gender perspective. These could be made available through the medium of radio. Many of the women entrepreneurs have radios at their places of work, and it is possible for them to listen to lessons while working. The programme should be designed to incorporate business management skills, as well as family and gender-related issues, such as the importance of family support for the success of a business; changing attitudes of husbands who become insecure due to success of the women; dealing with clients who insist on transacting with men, etc., and developing women's capacities to deal with such problems. The programme should also sensitize women on the need to socialize their children from an early age in their enterprise activities.

6.2.3 Researching and Documenting Strategies used by Successful Entrepreneurs

The strategies that have been adopted by the women entrepreneurs to help them to deal with challenges and achieve growth constitute a very relevant body of knowledge. A research programme should be launched to carefully study and systematically document the various strategies adopted by different women entrepreneurs who have become successful. Such knowledge should be published and shared widely, so that it is incorporated in various training and sensitization programmes for prospective as well as existing women entrepreneurs.

6.2.4 Improving Access to Finance for Growth-oriented MSEs

It is clear that growing MSEs, especially those owned by women, experience serious difficulties accessing finance, even when they have the potential to repay loans. It is recommended to introduce special means by which women who qualify for loans but lack collateral can access finance. Specifically, it is recommended to establish a Guarantee Fund for Women Entrepreneurs. A development agency could establish this fund in partnership with one or two local banks. Participating bank(s) could manage the fund. Such banks should be ones which have confidence to lend to MSEs, but fail to do so simply because MSEs lack the statutory collateral. The fund should build on the experiences of other guarantee schemes for SMEs, which have been operating in Tanzania.

6.2.5 Technical Skills Training in Beauty Care and Specialized Tailoring Skills

In order to fill the skills gap in these two areas, it is recommended that the Vocational Education and Training Authority (VETA) introduces relevant courses on beauty-care and specialized tailoring into their curricula. Support can be given in terms of experts and equipment to enable the VETA centres to introduce the courses. Further studies of other sectors might also reveal glaring skill gaps which need support under such a programme.

6.2.6 Improving Access to Premises for Women engaged in Food Processing

In order to enable women engaged in food processing to formalize and further expand their businesses, it is recommended to assist them by providing premises which they can rent at affordable rates, where they can set up their businesses formerly, and work there for a number of years while building their capacity to rent or build premises commercially. It is recommended that business incubators be established for those food-processing businesses with high growth potential. This can be done by building on the achievements of the UNIDO-supported food processing project, with further collaboration with the Ministry of Industry and Trade and the Small Industries Development Organization (SIDO) to identify appropriate land, service it and build the facilities required for this purpose. Some of the SIDO facilities currently being under-utilized could be rehabilitated for this purpose. Such facilities should be available in Dar es Salaam and other major business centres, such as Arusha. It would also be necessary to have different facilities created for different types of products.

6.2.7 Marketing Information and Advisory Services

It is recommended to establish marketing information and advisory services in different areas where MSEs are concentrated to promote the services offered by local business development services (BDS) providers. This should focus on developing local BDS providers' capacities to deliver their services, as well as to sell them to women in MSEs. Support should also be extended to make it possible for the BDS providers to gradually generate interest and willingness for local MSEs to pay for the service.

7. Recommendations from the National Stakeholders' Conference

A National Symposium on Women Entrepreneurs in Tanzania was organized by the ILO at Sea Cliff Hotel, Dar es Salaam, on 22 November 2002. More than 50 participants attended, including women entrepreneurs, representatives of women entrepreneurs' associations, and representatives from Government, NGOs and the donor community. All participants received a copy of the Preliminary Report on Tanzania (UDEC, 2002), as well as a set of the proposed support interventions as recommended by the team of national consultants. The second half of the Symposium was devoted to a participatory consultative process, in which participants had the opportunity to consider the research conclusions and proposals for supportive interventions. Through a group-work process, participants formulated four clusters of recommendations for follow-up action. These recommendations, which serve as a significant outcome from the ILO's research and consultation process, inform the ILO's ongoing and follow-up activities in support of women entrepreneurs in Tanzania. They also form the basis of an Action Programme that has been developed between ILO and the MIT SME Section.

7.1 Working Group on Business Associations

(a) Issues:

- Associations can act as important sources of support, developmental opportunities and advocacy mechanisms for women entrepreneurs.
- It is important for women entrepreneurs to join and to feel part of business associations, and in particular women entrepreneurs' associations, and to benefit from the wide range of services and support that can be provided by such associations. However, typically these associations do not have the necessary business skills to be able to provide all aspects of support. They should help their members to identify skill gaps and see if any of the members can provide these skills.
- Many associations are supply driven rather than demand driven, and they need to focus more on their members' needs. It is important that associations of women entrepreneurs should operate democratically and transparently and have good governance.

(b) Recommendations:

I. Associations need to promote awareness about themselves and the benefits they can bring to business by providing more information to a wider public about their organizations, their operations and their services. Information points should be established by the following organizations (some ministries and institutional service organizations were included in this list):

- Tanzania Chambers of Commerce Industry and Agriculture (TCCIA)
- Federation of Associations of Women Entrepreneurs in Tanzania (FAWETA)
- Tanzania Food Processing Association (TAFOPA)

- Small Industries Development Organization (SIDO)
- Tanzania Private Sector Foundation (TPSF)
- Tanzania Gender Networking Programme (TGNP)
- Ministry of Community Development, Women (Gender) and Children (MCDW/GC)
- International Labour Organization (ILO)

II.   Women entrepreneurs and associations of women entrepreneurs need to engage in more networking for their businesses, and use social events to enhance networking.

III.   There needs to be greater efforts made by associations to highlight and acknowledge all of their members' voices within the organizations. Capacity building support and guidance should be given to associations on issues such as democratic participation, governance and transparency in their operations provided.

III.   As most associations have inadequate capacities to deliver appropriate services to their members, there is a great and immediate need for capacity building and training, in particular in the fields of governance, leadership, communications and marketing.

IV.   As many associations are not well known, there is a need to carry out a marketing campaign and provide necessary training and capacity building for all associations.

V.   The creation of some form of network or forum between the different associations is also needed to help promote a collective voice and encourage inter-association development.

7.2   Working Group on Business Development Services (BDS)

(a)   Issues:

Payment for BDS is an issue as there is a tradition of providing free or subsidized services in Tanzania. In general, most women entrepreneurs are willing to pay for BDS, even if it is only a nominal amount. The key is to offer services and products that add value to clients' businesses and will encourage them to pay for BDS. BDS services – both in terms of what is offered and how it is offered – will need to be tailored to women entrepreneurs' needs, as these tend to be different from those of men.

(b)   Recommendations:

I.   Capacity building is needed for BDS providers, particularly in relation to the latest ideas on "market-oriented BDS" and sensitization on gender issues. A needs assessment should be carried out and recommendations on BDS product development and delivery mechanisms formulated by key actors.

II. Greater emphasis needs to be placed on information dissemination to ensure that BDS services are known to and address the needs of women entrepreneurs. It is necessary that private sector BDS providers, village councils, and others make effective use of the media to reach women entrepreneurs. Practical actions need to be developed as a matter of priority.

III. BDS providers should receive training and capacity building in gender mainstreaming and economic literacy. A wider range of training and support in women's entrepreneurship, business management, marketing, etc. should be offered by private sector BDS providers.

IV. BDS providers need to facilitate women entrepreneurs to become more competitive in the face of global competition, as this is placing severe economic pressure on women entrepreneurs throughout Tanzania.

7.3   Working Group on Financial Services

(a)   Issues:

Women entrepreneurs are potentially good customers for banks, but are not viewed as such by the lending institutions.

(b)   Recommendations:

I.   There is a need for banks to examine the market and segment the different needs and stages of development of a range of clients in the market. Based on this market analysis the banks should offer a wider range of interest rates to SMEs, including women entrepreneurs. This segmented approach could also help the Savings and Credit Cooperative Organizations' (SACCOs) review their lending capabilities in the light of the differing needs of various groups of women entrepreneurs.

II. Micro-finance institutions (MFIs) should carry out business analysis of the practical business needs of their customers so as to be able to formulate better and more appropriate modes of repayment. The main areas of concern and priority are:
- Often no grace period is provided for entrepreneurs, and the lending institutions should offer more flexibility on repayments.
- Loan durations are often too short for the needs of many women entrepreneurs. MFIs should introduce a wider range of loan repayment periods in response to differing needs.
- There is a gap between the provision of micro-level short-term loans and medium-term loans. It is recommended that MFIs introduce a wider range of loan sizes within their portfolios.

III. The current way in which collateral is demanded by the financial institutions tends to exclude (or at least discriminate against) women entrepreneurs more than men from obtaining loans. It is recommended that the government and MFIs should set out to tackle this by establishing mechanisms such as a guarantee fund to help women entrepreneurs to overcome this barrier.

IV. Women entrepreneurs need training from BDS providers to improve their skills in dealing with banks, preparing loan applications and managing money in a formal business context. Such training should build on the home-based cash management skills acquired by many women entrepreneurs. Providers of BDS should set out to deliver such financial capacity building as a matter of priority.

7.4 Working Group on the Business Environment

(a) Issues:

There are several key issues in the business environment that create undue problems and difficulties for women as opposed to men when it comes to starting and growing their own enterprises.

(b) Recommendations:

I. Women entrepreneurs need to have more and better access to information about their rights and entitlements, as well as about best practice models for women starting and running their own enterprises. It is recommended that a one-stop-shop solution could contribute to the provision of these supports and services.

II. Business registration procedures need to be tailored more effectively to the needs of MSEs, without any added burdens or bias affecting women entrepreneurs.

III. The issue of land ownership needs to be reviewed to remove customary gender-based loopholes from the law.

IV. Advocacy bodies and associations of women entrepreneurs need to work together to challenge prevailing cultural norms which result in men having greater (informal) control over resources.

V. As women experience particular difficulties in obtaining workspaces and business premises, the government should take actions to improve the supply of and access that women entrepreneurs have to appropriate and affordable premises.

Bibliography and Related References

Aboagye, A. A. 1985. An Analysis of the Dar es Salaam Informal Sector Survey, ILO, JASPA, Addis Ababa.

APDF, 2002. Survey of SMEs in Tanzania. Africa Project Development Facility Report Prepared by the University of Dar es Salaam Entrepreneurship Centre (UDEC).

Bagachwa, M. S. D. 1994. Poverty Alleviation in Tanzania: Recent Research Issues. Dar Es Salaam University Press.

Barwa, S. D., 2003, *Supporting Women in Enterprise in Vietnam: Impact of Start Your Business (SYB) Training on Women Entrepreneurs in Viet Nam*, Hanoi: ILO; Geneva: IFP/SEED-WEDGE.

Bendera, O. M. S. 1997. Micro and Small Enterprise Potential for Development: General Considerations. A Paper Presented to the workshop on Micro and Small Enterprise Research, November, Dar Es Salaam.

Bezhani, Mimoza, 2001. *Women Entrepreneurs in Albania.* Geneva: ILO, IFP/SEED-WEDGE Working Paper No. 21.

Bol, D. 1995. Employment and Equity Issues in Tanzania In Msambichaka, L.A., A. A. Akilindo, and G. D. Mjema (eds.) Beyond Structural Adjustments Programme in Tanzania, Successes, Failures and New Perspectives, Economic Research Bureau, University of Dar es Salaam.

Buberwa, S. B. and A. I. Mdamo 1991. Tanzania: The informal sector 1991, Mimeo, Dar es Salaam, Government of Tanzania/ILO.

Buckley, G. 1997. Microfinance in Africa: Is it Either the Problem of the Solution. World Development, Vol. 25, No. 7, pp. 1081-1093.

Bwisa, H. M. 1998. Demand–driven MSE Research in Kenya: Critical Issues. A background paper Presented to the Kenyan National Workshop on MSE Demand-Driven Research Organized by FIT and Sponsored by ILO: Mayfair Hotel, Nairobi. January.

Chijoriga, M. M. 2000. Performance and Sustainability of Micro Financing Schemes in Tanzania. The Austrian Journal of Development Studies, Volume, XVI/3, December.

Chijoriga, M. M. 1997. Potentials and Limitations of Micro and Small Enterprise (MSEs) Financing Options in Tanzania – in the proceedings of the 4th International Conference on Modernisation and Management Entebbe Uganda, Faculty of Commerce University of Makerere Uganda.

Chijoriga, M.M. and D. Cassimon 1999. Micro-enterprise Financing: Is There a Best Model? in Rutashobya and Olomi (eds.). African Entrepreneurship and Small Business Management, DUP, Dar Es Salaam.

Dar es Salaam Informal Sector Survey 1995.

Davidsson, 1998. Continued Entrepreneurship and Small Firm Growth Ph.D dissertation, Stockholm School of Economics.

ESRF, 2001. Do Decent Jobs Require Good Policies? A Case Study of MSEs in Tanzania, Final Report by the Economic and Social Research Foundation, Dar es Salaam, Tanzania.

Essoo, Venda, *Promoting Female Entrepreneurship in Mauritius: Strategies in Training and Development.* Geneva: ILO, IFP/SEED-WEDGE Working Paper (forthcoming).

Ferdinand, Carol (ed.), 2001. *Jobs, Gender and Small Enterprises in the Caribbean: Lessons from Barbados, Suriname and Trinidad and Tobago.* Geneva: ILO, IFP/SEED-WEDGE Working Paper No. 19.

Finseth, W. 1998. A Strategic Plan To develop Tanzania's National Policy Framework For Small Business.

Goheer, Nabeel A., 2003, *Women Entrepreneurs in Pakistan: How to improve their bargaining power.* Islamabad: ILO; Geneva: IFP/SEED-WEDGE.

Hanna-Andesson, C. 1995. SIDA's support to Women Small Scale Enterprises in Tanzania In L. Dinged and J. Haft (Des) Women in MSEs Development. IT publication, UK.

Hulme, D. and Michael E. 1996. Too Close for Comfort? The Impact of Official Aid on NGOs World development, pp. 961-71.

Hulme, D. and Mosley P. 1998. Micro-enterprise Finance: Is There a Conflict Between Growth and Poverty Alleviation? World development Journal Vol. 26, No. 5, pp. 783-790.

Hulme, D. and Mosley P. 1996a. Finance Against Poverty, Volume I, Routledge.

Hulme, D. and Mosley P.1996b. Finance Against Poverty, Volume II, Routledge.

ILO, 2003, *Ethiopian Women Entrepreneurs: Going for Growth.* Geneva: ILO, IFP/SEED-WEDGE (forthcoming).

ILO, 2003, *Zambian Women Entrepreneurs: Going for Growth.* Geneva: ILO, IFP/SEED-WEDGE (forthcoming).

ILO, 2003, *L'entreprenariat feminine dans les îles de l'océan Indien*. Antananarivo: ILO (forthcoming).

ILO, 2002, *Promoting Women's Entrepreneurship through Employers' Organizations in the Asia-Pacific Region: Final Report. October 2002.* Geneva: ILO, IFP/SEED-WEDGE.

ILO, 2002, *Promoting Women's Entrepreneurship through Employers' Organizations in the Asia-Pacific Region: Final Report. Annexes: Presentations and Papers. October 2002.* Geneva: ILO, IFP/SEED-WEDGE.

ILO, 2000. State of the Art Review of the Tanzanian Informal Sector. This was a review of needs, constraints and services available in the informal sector, with a particular emphasis on problems facing women.

ILO, 2001. The influence of national policies, laws and regulations on employment in MSEs.

ILO, UNDP, UNIDO (2001). Final Draft RoadMap Informal Sector Study for Tanzania: Why MSEs find Formalisation Daunting. Dar es Salaam, October.

JUDAI & Associates, 2002, *Jobs, Gender and Small Enterprises in Africa: Women Entrepreneurs in Zambia.* A Preliminary Report. Geneva: IFP/SEED-WEDGE, October.

Kantor, Paula, 2000. *Promoting Women's Entrepreneurship Development based on Good Practice Programmes: Some Experiences from the North to the South.* Geneva: ILO, IFP/SEED-WEDGE Working Paper No. 9.

Karim, Nilufer Ahmed, 2001. *Jobs, Gender and Small Enterprises in Bangladesh: Factors Affecting Women Entrepreneurs in Small and Cottage Industries in Bangladesh.* Geneva: ILO, IFP/SEED-WEDGE Working Paper No. 14.

Kombe, Z. 1994. The Problems Faced by Married Women in Business in Besha, R.M.(ed.) African Women: Our Burdens and Struggles. Institute of African Alternatives pp.12-18.

Labour Force Survey 1991. Planning Commission, Dar es Salaam.

Malima, R. 1997. Pride Tanzania: Experience in Micro Finance Initiatives. The Tanzanian Bankers Journal. Issue No. 9, June.

Marcucci, Pamela Nichols 2001. *Jobs, Gender and Small Enterprises in Africa and Asia: Lessons drawn from Bangladesh, the Philippines, Tunisia and Zimbabwe.* Geneva: ILO, IFP/SEED-WEDGE Working Paper No. 18.

Mayoux, Linda, 2001. *Jobs, Gender and Small Enterprises: Getting the Policy Environment Right.* Geneva: ILO, IFP/SEED-WEDGE Working Paper No. 15

Mbuguni, P. and S. Mwangunga 1998. The Integration of Women into Small Scale Industrial Sector A report prepared for SIDO and SIDA, Dar es Salaam.
National Informal Sector Survey 1991.

Nchimbi, M. 2000. "A Comparison of Male and Female Personal Characteristics, Start-up Motives and Perception of Success", paper presented at the International Conference on African Entrepreneurship and Small Business Development, Dar es Salaam.

Olomi D. and N. Mbise 2001. Baseline Survey of members of Tanzania Food Processing Association (TAFOPA).

Olomi, D. R. 2001. Incidence, Antecedents and Consequences of Growth-seeking Behaviour Among Tanzanian Owner-Managers". Ph.D. dissertation, University of Dar es Salaam.

Rahman A. 1999. Micro-Credit Initiatives for Equitable and Sustainable Development: Who Pays?. World Development, Vol. 27, No. 1, pp. 67-82.

RPED 1996. Regional Program on Enterprise Development. Development and Growth of Industrial Enterprises in Tanzania – Phase III. Centre for International Business Research, Helsinki School of Economics, Helsinki.

Rutashobya, L. K. 1991.Credit Acquisition by Women in the Informal Sector: The Role of Women Co-operatives in Tanzania. Research Report, African Training and Research Centre for Women, UNECA, Addis.

Rutashobya, L. 1995. Women in Business: Entry and Performance Barriers. Unpublished Research Report, University of Dar es Salaam.

Rutashobya, L., and M. Nchimbi 1998: The African Female Entrepreneur: Knowledge, Gaps and Priority Areas for Future Research, in African Entrepreneurship and Small Business Development, ed. by L. K.

Rutashobya, and D. R. Olomi. Dar es Salaam: DUP Ltd.

Rutashobya L. and Olomi D. 1999. African Entrepreneurship and Small Business Management, DUP, Dar Es Salaam.

Stoyanovska, Antonina, 2001. Jobs, Gender and Small Enterprises in Bulgaria. Geneva: ILO, IFP/SEED-WEDGE Working Paper No. 20.

Swai Riordan, J. F. and A. Rugumyamheto 1997. Educational Background, Training and their Influence on Female-operated Informal Sector Enterprises. Research on Poverty Alleviation (REPOA), Research Report No. 97.3.

Temu, S. L. 1998. "Gender and Small Industry in Tanzania," University of Liepzig *Papers, Politics and Economics* No. 16.

Toroka, E. B. and Wenga 1997. Small Industries Development Organization: Tanzania Experience with MSE Development. A Paper Presented to the workshop on Micro and Small Enterprise Research, November, Dar Es Salaam.

University of Dar es Salaam Entrepreneurship Centre (UDEC), 2002, *Jobs, Gender and Small Enterprises in Africa: Women Entrepreneurs in Tanzania.* A Preliminary Report. Geneva: ILO, IFP/SEED-WEDGE, October.

University of Oxford/ESRF, 1998. Survey of small manufacturing enterprises in Tanzania. Unpublished report. Dar es Salaam.

URT, 2000a. Tanzania Poverty Reduction Strategy Paper, Dar es Salaam, Tanzania: The United Republic of Tanzania.

URT, 2000b. Women Credit Facility in Tanzania.

URT,2000c. Optimal Modalities Towards Increasing the Access of the Poor to Micro-Credit Facilities.

USAID, 2001. Baseline survey of SME activities in Mbeya, Ruvuma, Tanga, Iringa, and Rukwa.

Verspreet, D. and L. Berlage 1999. Small Scale Enterprise Development in Tanzania: Driving Forces, Research report, Faculty of Economic and Applied Economic Science, Centre for Economic Studies. KUL.

World Bank, 2001. Country SME Map – Tanzania.

Zewde & Associates, 2002, *Jobs, Gender and Small Enterprises in Africa: Women Entrepreneurs in Ethiopia.* A Preliminary Report, Geneva: ILO, IFP/SEED-WEDGE, October.

Annex 1

IFP/SEED's WED RESEARCH PROJECT
Gender, Jobs and Small Enterprise in Africa

QUESTIONNAIRE FOR TANZANIAN WOMEN ENTREPRENEURS

Note: The respondent must be the owner-manager (one who makes major decisions in the business)

Date of interview:	dd_____mm_____yy_____
Interviewer's name:	

QUALITY CONTROL *[To be filled in by supervisor after interview]*

Checked by:		Corrected	Yes	No
Date checked:				
Country:				

RESPONDENT CRITERIA

Please ensure that the respondent meets the criteria by asking:	Yes	No
Are you the owner of this business?	1	2
Do you have a major role in making important decisions in this business?	1	2
Has this business been operating for at least two years?	1	2
Have you been the owner-manager of this business over the last two years?	1	2
Did you start this business?	1	2

Type of business:		Size:	Micro	1
Sector:			Small	2

PART I: PROFILE OF THE ENTREPRENEUR

1. General information

(a) Age (in years) - select one:

1	Below 20	4	20 to 30
2	31 to 40	5	41 to 50
3	51 to 60	6	Over 60

(b) Marital status:

	Before starting business	Currently
Married	1	1
Single	2	2
Separated	3	3
Divorced	4	4
Widowed	5	5

(c) Owner's level of education
Highest level of education attained (please, mark one)

Never attended formal education	1
Primary school	2
O-Level secondary school	3
A-Level secondary school	4
Post-secondary certificate	5
Ordinary diploma	6
Advanced Diploma/First degree	7
(8) ___ Postgraduate qualification	8
Other (please, specify)	9

Highest specific professional qualification attained (e.g. Bachelor of Commerce in marketing, Certificate in teacher education, etc.)_____

2. Family Background

(a) What is the level of education completed by the following members of your family (please tick one)

	spouse	father	mother
Never attended formal education	1	1	1
Primary school	2	2	2
O-Level secondary school	3	3	3
A-Level secondary school	4	4	4
Post-secondary certificate	5	5	5
Ordinary diploma	6	6	6
Advanced Diploma/First degree	7	7	7
Postgraduate qualification	8	8	8
Not applicable	9	9	9
Other (please, specify)			

(b) Kindly provide the following information

    1.   Father's main occupation: _____

    2.   Mother's main occupation: _____

    3.   Spouse's main occupation: _____

(c) Do you have children?   Yes [1]   No [2]

If yes, how many children do you have?

	Age			
Girls				
Boys				

(d) What kind of family structure are you living in

Nuclear family	1
Extended family	2
Alone	3
Other (specify)	4

3. Previous experience

What were you doing immediately before starting this business? (please tick one)

1	Student	4	In another business (specify)
2	Employed	5	Unemployed
3	Housewife	6	Other (specify)

If you had been employed at any point in time, please indicate your employment history below. If you have not been employed proceed to the next question.		
From (year)	*To (year)*	*Job title*

4. Have you had, or do you currently run another business apart from this one? Yes [1] No.[2] If yes, kindly indicate the type, year of establishment, whether or not the business still exists and number of people employed by completing the following. Otherwise proceed to the next question.			
Type of business	Year Established	Year discontinued	Maximum number of people ever employed

PART II: PROFILE OF THE ENTERPRISE

1. (a) Legal status of business when it started and now (select one each side):

	When it started:	Now:
Sole proprietorship	1	1
Partnership	2	2
Limited Liability Company	3	3
Other (please specify		

2. Business Licence

(a) What type of licence, if any did you have when the business started and what type of licence do you have now for this business?

	When the Business Started	Currently
No licence	1	1
Minor licence	2	2
Principal licence	3	3

If you currently have a principal licence, proceed to question 3.

(b) If you currently have no principal licence, what are the reasons?

(c) Do you plan to have one in the future? Yes [1] No [2]. If Yes, When: mm _____ yy 20____

(d) If you currently have a minor licence, why have you not sought a principal licence?

3. How many owners are there in *this* business? _____

4. Year of establishment and location:

When was the business established?:   Year _____   Month_____

Location   Region _____ District_____

5. Main products/services of the business

When the business started: Currently:

1._____   1._____

2._____   2._____

3._____   3._____

6. Premises
From where did you operate this business when it started and from where do you operate it now?

	When It Started:	**Currently:**
Business premises owned by you	1	1
Rented business premises	2	2
Home	3	3
Other (specify)		

7. Please, indicate the approximate number of people working in this business (including owners regularly working for the business, when it started and now

	When business started		At present	
	women	men	women	men
1. Full-time[5]				
2. Part-time[6]				
3. Paid family members				
4. Unpaid family members				
5. Apprentices				
6. Casual/temporary				

8. Please indicate whether you provided the following benefits to your employees when the business started, now and whether you plan to provide them in the future

	When the business started		**Now**		**In the future**	
1. Written employment contracts	Yes [1]	No [2]	Yes [1]	No [2]	Yes [1]	No [2]
2. Pension contributions	1	2	1	2	1	2
3. Maternity leave	1	2	1	2	1	2
4. Annual leave	1	2	1	2	1	2

9. How did you finance your business at the start and how do you finance it now? (Select all applicable)

Source:	**At start**	**Now**
My own savings	1	1
Credit from a bank	2	2
Credit from a Micro-Finance Institution (MFIs)	3	3
Credit from friend or family members	4	4
Credit from private money lender	5	5

10. How much was the approximate value of cash, equipment, and inventory when the business started and how much is it now?

	When the Business Started	Currently
1. Approximate amount of cash	Tshs.	Tshs.
2. Approximate value of equipment		
3. Approximate value of inventory		

11. Bank Account
Did you have a bank account(s) for the business in the first 12 months of the business and do you have one now?

Type of Account	**Within the first 12 months of the business**	**Currently**
Savings Account (How many?)		
Current Account (How many?)		

---

[5] Working at least for the normal working time for the business
[6] Working for less that the normal working time for the business

PART III: STARTING AND DEVELOPING THE BUSINESS

1. What were the most important reasons to start <u>this business?</u> (up to 3)
1.
2.
3.

2. What were the major factors that were helpful in starting this business (up to 3)
1.
2.
3.

3. What were the main problems faced in starting this business?
1.
2.
3.

4. Did you experience any problems when you started this business? Yes [1] No [2] If the answer is No, proceed to Question 6.

5. If you experienced problems, were these related to your being a women? Yes [1] No [2]
If the answer is yes, explain how?

6. What was your main role in the business when it started and what is your main role now?

	When the business started	Currently
Doing the work in the business	1	1
Assigning work and supervising employees to do the work	2	2
Overseeing supervisors/managers	3	3

7. What are your plans for this business in the next five years? (Please select one)

Continue with the business at the same size	1	Go to Qn. 8
Slightly increase the size of the business	2	
Significantly increase the size of the business	3	
Significantly reduce the size of the business	4	
Change to another line of business	5	
Leave the business and take up wage employment	6	
Start another business and keep the present one	7	
Start several other businesses and keep the present one	8	
Pass the business onto someone else in my family	9	
Sell the business	10	
Hire a manager	11	
Retire	12	
Other (specify)	13	

8. If you plan to continue with business how do you expect <u>to continue</u> it over the next one year? (If you do not plan to continue with it, proceed to question 9, others fill N/A)

		Yes	No	N/A
1	No changes planned	1	2	3
2	Make new investments in the business	1	2	3
3	Increase the number of workers	1	2	3
4	Decrease the number of workers	1	2	3
5	Expand the range of products/service	1	2	3
6	Reduce the range of products/services	1	2	3
7	Don't know	1	2	3
8	Other (specify)	1	2	3

9. How much was the approximate value of your sales/revenue in the first financial year and how were your sales/revenues in the last financial year.

	1st Financial Year	Last Financial Year
Sales in Tshs		

10. Please, indicate in which markets you sold most of your products when the business started, in which markets do you sell most of them now and in which markets do you expect to sell most of them in the future:

Markets	When the business started		Now		In the future	
1. Local markets (within the district)	Yes [1]	No [2]	Yes [1]	No [2]	Yes [1]	No [2]
2. Regional markets (in more than one district)	1	2	1	2	1	2
3. International markets (outside the country)	1	2	1	2	1	2

11. Which of the following do your prefer?

To have one business that develops to a medium or large enterprise	1
To have many microenterprises	2
To have many small & medium businesses !!	3
No preference	4
Other (please specify)	5

12. If the firm develops the way you would like it to, how many employees (both full-time and part-time) would the firm have five years from now? _____ employees.

13. What are the most important factors that can help your business to grow? (up to 3)

1.	
2.	
3.	

14. Are there any barriers to growth of the business? Yes [1] No [2]
15. If the answer to question 14 is yes, what do you consider to be the most significant barriers to the growth of your business? (up to 3)

1.	
2.	
3.	

PART III: BUSINESS ENVIRONMENT AND SUPPORT SERVICES

1. Does the business environment discriminate against small businesses?
   Yes [1] No [2]. If the answer is yes, explain how?

2. Are there situations where the business environment affects women entrepreneurs more than their male counterparts? Yes [1] No [2]. If the answer is Yes, explain how

3. Are you aware of any policies or regulations that affect women owned enterprises negatively?
   Yes [1] No [2].   If yes, mention these policies (if no, proceed to question 5):

4. If there are policies or regulations that affect women owned enterprises, what changes are needed in these policies or regulations in order to make them more friendly to women owned enterprises?

   1._____

   2._____

5. From your experience, are there any government regulations that were difficult to comply with? Yes [1] No [2]. If no, proceed to question 8. If yes, which policies or regulations?

   1._____

   2._____

6. If Yes, did you manage to comply with these regulations or policies? Yes [1] No [2]

7. If yes to Qn 6., how did you manage to comply with the regulations and policies that were difficult to comply with?

   1._____

   2._____

8. Please, describe two critical incidents that have negatively impacted on your business since you started:
   1. _____
   2. _____

9. Have you tried to access a loan from any of the following sources. If so, were you successful? *(Please fill the table below)*

Source	Tried to access credit?		Successful?	
	Yes	No	Yes	No
1. Bank	1	2	1	2
2. Micro-Finance Institution (MFIs)	1	2	1	2
3. Friend and Family members	1	2	1	2
4. Money lender	1	2	1	2
5. Other (specify)..	1	2	1	2

10. If you have obtained credit, please show the source of each loan you have obtained, the amount, year obtained and purpose for which it was taken

Source of Credit [Name of the institution]	Amount	Year Obtained	Purpose

11. If you tried to access a loan and you were unsuccessful, why were you unsuccessful?

1._____

2._____

12. If you have not tried to get a loan, why?

1._____

2._____

13. Does your being a woman make its more difficult for you to get a loan?

Yes	How?
No	Why

14. Have you faced any problems in borrowing money? Yes [1] No [2]. If the answer is yes, which problems did you face? (select all applicable)

Cumbersome procedures (please, specify)	1
High interest rates	2
Small loan sizes offered by Micro Finance Institutions	3
Lack of collateral	4
Inability to write business plans	5
Other (specify)	6

15. Have you received any business support (advise, marketing, technology, legal, technical) since you started this business? Yes [1] No [2]. If the answer is No, proceed to Question 17. If the answer is Yes, complete the following table.

Support/Services	Name of Providing Institution

16. Are there any improvements in your business performance which is associated with the services that you mentioned? Yes [1] No [2]. If the answer is no, proceed to question 17. If the answer is Yes, complete the following table

Suport/Services and Institution Providing Them	Improvements in the Business as a Result of the Support

17. To what extent are you aware of the following associations?

Association	Have you heard of it?		Do you know its objectives?		Are you a member?	
	Yes	No	Yes	No	Yes	No
Viwanda na Biashara Ndogondogo (VIBINDO)	1	2	1	2	1	2
Tanzania Chamber of Commerce, Industry and Agriculture (TCCIA)	1	2	1	2	1	2
Tanzania Federation of Women Entrepreneurs (FAWETA)	1	2	1	2	1	2
Tanzania Food Processors Association (TAFOPA)	1	2	1	2	1	2
Tanzania Private Sector Foundation (TPSF)	1	2	1	2	1	2
National Business Council (NBC)	1	2	1	2	1	2

18. If you are a member of any of these associations, what services have you obtained from it/them?

    1._____

    2._____

    3. _____

19. If you are not a member of any of the associations mentioned in Question 17 above, explain why?

    1._____

    2._____

20. What do you think about the outreach, range of services and performance of women business associations in Tanzania (tick the appropriate box).

	Outreach	Range of Services	Performance
Good	1	1	1
Average	2	2	2
Bad	3	3	3
Don't know	4	4	4

PART VI: WILLINGNESS TO PARTICIPATE IN AN IN DEPTH STUDY

The researchers would like to visit some women and discuss in detail their experiences and problems in order to get a better/deeper understanding of problems facing women entrepreneurs in Tanzania. During these discussions, they will also advise you on any areas that you wish to be advised. Are you interested to be visited by the researchers for more detailed discussions? Yes [1]   No [2]

THANK YOU VERY MUCH FOR YOUR CO-OPERATION

Annex 2: In-depth Interview Guide

1. **Motivation to start business**
   - Conditions leading to involvement in each business ever started by the respondent
   - Primary reason for starting each business ever started by the respondent
   - Other reasons for starting each business
   - Benefits derived from the business when it started and how this has been changing over time
   - Benefits derived from the business now
   - The most valued among the benefits obtained from the business when it started and how this has been changing over time?
   - The most valued among benefits obtained from doing business now
   - What doing business meant to the respondent when he/she started business and how this has changed over time?
   - What doing each specific type of business meant to the respondent when he/she started doing business and how this has changed over time?

2. **Process of starting and developing business**
   - How did it start (formal, informal, micro, serious business etc) and why?
   - Who facilitated the set-up and how?
   - How did it become formal? How has formalization helped/hindered?
   - How did it grow?

3. **Progressions/ Developments/ Changes/ Transitions**
   - Progressions/ developments in business (both negative and positive) that have taken place over the course of each of the businesses
   - Whether/ which of the developments were deliberately sought before they occurred
   - Whether the owner had a conscious strategy for achieving each of the developments
   - Explanation for progressions/ developments that have taken place in the business (What lead to each of the (positive and negative) developments?
   - Developments (negative and positive) in the respondent's intentions about the business
   - Whether one has clear/ growth intentions or clear strategy for growth
   - Future growth aspirations with each of the businesses owned
   - Explanations/ reasons for specific aspirations

4. **Challenges and how they were dealt with**
   - Challenges that the business has faced (internal and external)
   - How have the challenges impacted the business and the owners?
   - How have the challenges been managed ?
   - Any challenge associated with being a woman
   - Any challenges associated with being married/ family
   - Any advantages in business from being a woman

5. **The Future**
   - Future intentions and reasons for these
   - Expectations (opportunities, problems) how they match with the intentions and reasons for differences

6. **Lessons from the woman's experience**
   - What can other women learn from her experience? Can it be "learnt" ?
   - What can BDS providers, local government, central government do to help out women entrepreneurs

Annex 3.1: Age, Education and Experience by Sector and Location

	Dar es Salaam (%) N=24				Arusha (%) N=39				Zanzibar (%) N=24				Total N = 128
	TT	FP	HB	Total	TT	FP	HB	Total	TT	FP	HB	Total	
Age													
Below 20	-	1.5	-	1.5	-	-	-	-	-	-	-	-	0.8
20-30 years	15.4	-	9.2	24.6	5.1	-	10.3	15.4	4.2	8.3	4.2	16.7	20.3
31-40 years	16.9	10.8	10.8	38.5	20.5	10.3	12.8	43.6	12.5	8.3	20.8	41.7	40.6
41-50 years	13.8	10.8	3.1	27.7	15.4	15.4	7.7	38.5	16.7	8.3	-	25.0	30.5
Over 50 years	-	6.1	-	6.1	2.6	-	-	2.6	4.2	12.5	-	16.7	7.0
Non-response	-	1.5	-	1.5	-	-	-	-	-	-	-	-	0.8
Total	46.2	30.8	23.1	100	43.6	25.6	30.8	100	37.5	37.5	25.0	100	100.0
Level of Education													
Never attended	-	-	-	-	-	-	-	-	-	4.2	-	4.2	0.8
Primary school	23.1	4.6	3.1	30.8	10.3	2.6	-	12.8	16.7	25.0	-	41.7	27.3
O-Level Secondary	9.2	12.3	12.3	33.8	15.4	5.1	23	43.6	12.5	8.3	20.8	41.7	38.3
A-Level Secondary	3.1	-	3.1	6.2	2.6	2.6	2.6	7.7	-	-	-	-	5.5
Post-secondary certificate	4.6	6.2	4.6	15.4	5.1	10.3	2.6	17.9	4.2	-	-	4.2	14.1
Ordinary Diploma	4.6	6.2	-	10.8	10.3	2.6	2.6	15.4	4.2	-	4.2	8.3	11.7
Advanced diploma/Degree	1.5	-	-	1.5	-	-	-	-	-	-	-	-	0.8
No response	-	1.5	-	1.5	-	2.6	-	2.6	-	-	-	-	1.6
Total	46.2	30.8	23.1	100.0	43.6	25.6	30.8	100	37.5	37.5	25.0	100	100.0
Work Experience													
Student	6.2	-	9.2	15.4	2.6	-	2.6	5.1	12.5	-	4.2	16.7	12.5
Employed	20.0	21.5	10.8	52.3	30.8	23.1	17.9	71.8	12.5	12.5	4.2	29.2	53.9
Housewife	9.2	-	-	9.2	-	-	2.6	2.6	4.2	8.3	-	12.5	7.8
In another business	6.2	9.2	1.5	16.9	7.7	2.6	2.6	12.8	8.3	16.7	12.5	37.5	19.5
Unemployed	4.6	-	1.5	6.2	2.6	-	2.6	5.1	-	-	4.2	4.2	5.5
Non-response	-	-	-	-	-	-	2.6	2.6	-	-	-	-	0.8
Total	46.2	30.8	23.1	100.0	43.6	25.6	30.8	100.0	37.5	37.5	25.0	100.0	100.0

Annex 3.2: Education Level by the Members of the Family by Sector and Location

SPOUSE	Dar es Salaam		Arusha		Zanzibar		Total	
	Number	%	Number	%	Number	%	Number	%
Non Response	7	5.5					7	5.5
Never attended formal education					2	1.6	2	1.6
Primary school	5	3.9	-	-	4	3.1	9	7.0
O-Level secondary school	13	10.2	13	10.2	11	8.6	37	28.9
A-Level secondary school	1	0.8	1	0.8	-	-	2	1.6
Post secondary certificate	4	3.1	4	3.1	1	0.8	9	7.0
Ordinary diploma	5	3.9	7	5.5	-	-	12	9.4
Advanced diploma/First Degree	11	8.6	4	3.1	1	0.8	16	12.5
Postgraduate Qualification	10	7.8	4	3.1	2	1.6	16	12.5
Not Applicable	9	7.0	6	4.7	3	2.3	18	14.1
Total	65	50.8	39	30.5	24	18.8	128	100.0

FATHER	Dar es Salaam		Arusha		Zanzibar		Total	
	Number	%	Number	%	Number	%	Number	%
Non Response	4	3.1					4	3.1
Never attended formal education	4	3.1	7	5.5	9	7.0	20	15.6
Primary school	27	21.1	11	8.6	10	7.8	48	37.5
O-Level secondary school	6	4.7	6	4.7	3	2.3	15	11.7
A-Level secondary school	1	0.8	-	-	-	-	1	0.8
Post secondary certificate	4	3.1	1	0.8	1	0.8	6	4.7
Ordinary diploma	3	2.3	1	0.8	-	-	4	3.1
Advanced diploma/First Degree	3	2.3	2	1.6	1	0.8	6	4.7
Postgraduate Qualification	2	1.6	-	-	-	-	2	1.6
Not Applicable	5	3.9	-	-	-	-	5	3.9
Standard 8	6	4.7	11	8.6	-	-	17	13.3
Total	65	50.8	39	30.5	24	18.8	128	100.0

MOTHER	Dar es Salaam		Arusha		Zanzibar		Total	
	Number	%	Number	%	Number	%	Number	%
Non Response	3	2.3	-	-	-	-	3	2.3
Never attended formal education	15	11.7	8	6.3	16	12.5	39	30.5
Primary school	27	21.1	20	15.6	7	5.5	54	42.2
O-Level secondary school	9	7.0	4	3.1	1	0.8	14	10.9
Ordinary diploma	3	2.3	1	0.8	-	-	4	3.1
Not Applicable	3	2.3	-	-	-	-	3	2.3
Standard 8	5	3.9	6	4.7	-	-	11	8.6
Total	65	50.8	39	30.5	24	18.8	128	100.0

Annex 3.3 Type of Family by Sector and Location

		Food processing		Health and Beauty		Textile		Total	
		Number	%	Number	%	Number	%	Number	%
Dar es Salaam	Nuclear family	2	3.1	1	1.5	7	10.8	10	15.4
	Extended family	12	18.5	8	12.3	19	29.2	39	60.0
	Alone	-	-	5	7.7	2	3.1	7	10.8
	Mother and children	6	9.2	1	1.5	1	1.5	8	12.3
	Living with parents/relative	-	-	-	-	1	1.5	1	1.5
	Total	**20**	**30.8**	**15**	**23.1**	**30**	**46.2**	**65**	**100.0**
Arusha	Non response	-	-	1	2.6	-	-	1	2.6
	Nuclear family	3	7.7	4	10.3	3	7.7	10	25.6
	Extended family	6	15.4	6	15.4	11	28.2	23	59.0
	Alone	-	-	1	2.6	1	2.6	2	5.1
	Mother and children	1	2.6	-	-	2	5.1	3	7.7
	Total	**10**	**25.6**	**12**	**30.8**	**17**	**43.6**	**39**	**100.0**
Zanzibar	Non response	-	-	1	4.2	-	-	1	4.2
	Nuclear family	2	8.3	2	8.3	3	12.5	7	29.2
	Extended family	3	12.5	1	4.2	4	16.7	8	33.3
	Alone	-	-	1	4.2	-	-	1	4.2
	Mother and children	3	12.5	1	4.2	2	8.3	6	25.0
	Living with parents/relative	1	4.2	-	-	-	-	1	4.2
	Total	**9**	**37.5**	**6**	**25.0**	**9**	**37.5**	**24**	**100.0**

Annex 3.4 Year of Establishment by Sector and Location

	Dar es Salaam % N = 65				Arusha % N = 39				Zanzibar % N = 24				Total N = 128
	TT	FP	HB	Total	TT	FP	HB	Total	TT	FP	HB	Total	
Before 1985	0	1.5	-	1.5	5.1	-	-	5.1	8.3	16.7	-	25.0	7.0
1986-1994	12.3	3.1	1.5	16.9	7.7	5.1	7.7	20.5	8.3	8.3	4.2	20.8	18.8
1995-1999	21.5	13.8	15.4	50.8	25.6	15.4	23.1	64.1	16.7	12.5	20.8	50.0	54.7
2000	12.3	10.8	4.6	27.7	5.1	5.1	-	10.3	4.2	-	-	4.2	18.0
Non-Response	-	1.5	1.5	3.1	-	-	-	-	-	-	-	-	1.6
Total	46.2	30.8	23.1	100.0	43.6	25.6	30.8	100.0	37.5	37.5	25.0	100.0	100.0

FP= Food Processing; HB= Health and Beauty; TT= Textile

Annex 3.5 Number of Workers (Including the Owner) by Sector and Location

Number	Dar es Salaam % N=65				Arusha % N=39				Zanzibar % N=24				Total N=128
	FP	HB	TT	Total	FP	HB	TT	Total	FP	HB	TT	Total	
1-5	15.4	13.8	23.1	52.3	7.7	17.9	15.4	41.0	12.5	25	20.8	58.3	50.0
6-9	6.2	4.6	10.8	21.5	10.3	-	5.1	15.4	8.3	-	-	8.3	17.2
10-20	9.2	4.6	7.7	21.5	2.6	7.7	17.9	28.2	16.7	-	16.7	33.3	25.8
>20	-	-	4.6	4.6	5.1	-	2.6	7.7	-	-	-	-	4.7
Non response	-	-	-	-	-	5.1	-	7.7	-	-	-	-	2.3
Total	30.8	23.1	46.2	100	25.6	30.8	43.6	100	37.5	25.0	37.5	100	100

FP= Food Processing; HB= Health and Beauty; TT= Textile

Annex 3.6 Sources of Finance when the Business Started and Currently by Sector and Location

Source of finance	When business started N=128				Currently N=128			
	Dar es Salaam	Arusha	Zanzibar	Total	Dar es Salaam	Arusha	Zanzibar	Total
Own saving	32.8	25.0	9.4	67.2	35.2	25.8	18.0	78.9
Credit from bank	1.6	2.3	-	3.9	3.1	7.0	-	10.2
Credit from MFIs	4.7	2.3	1.6	8.6	12.5	10.9	1.6	25.0
Credit from friends and family	16.4	3.1	1.6	21.1	9.4	3.1	0	12.5
From private money lenders	-	-	0.8	0.8	0.8	0.8	-	1.6
Assistance from husband	15.6	12.5	4.7	32.8	0.8	0.8	-	1.6

Annex 3.7 Growth Aspirations in Terms of Employment Size

	Total Employees Currently	Growth aspiration									
		Non Response		1 to 9		10 to 19		20 to 50		Total	
		Number	%	Number	%	Number	%	Number	%	Number	%
Food processing	1 to 4	2	5.1	10	25.6	4	10.3	2	5.1	18	46.2
	5 to 10	2	5.1	-	-	15	38.5	2	5.1	19	48.7
	11 to 15	-	-	-	-	-	-	2	5.1	2	5.1
	Total	4	10.3	10	25.6	19	48.7	6	15.4	39	100.0
Health and Beauty	1 to 4	3	9.1	17	51.5	3	9.1	-	-	23	69.7
	5 to 10	-	-	1	3.0	5	15.2	-	-	6	18.2
	11 to 15	1	3.0	1	3.0	2	6.1	-	-	4	12.1
	Total	4	12.1	19	57.6	10	30.3	-	-	33	100.0
Textile	1 to 4	4	7.1	19	33.9	4	7.1	1	1.8	28	50.0
	5 to 10	-	-	4	7.1	8	14.3	6	10.7	18	32.1
	11 to 15	1	1.8	-	-	-	-	6	10.7	7	12.5
	Over 15	-	-	-	-	-	-	3	5.4	3	5.4
	Total	5	8.9	23	41.1	12	21.4	16	28.6	56	100.0